Heartbeats:
True Stories of Love

Compiled by Lynda Freeman
manyheartbeats@gmail.com

*Heartbeats, True Stories of Love*
Copyright 2014 by Lynda Freeman
All rights reserved
Published by Lynda Freeman

Library and Archives Canada Cataloguing in
Publication
Information is available upon request

ISBN 978-0-9939755-0-9

Designed by Brian Boutin
Edited by Sharon Crawford

*Only love interests me, and I am only in contact with things that revolve around love.*
*In our life there is a single color, as on an artist's palette, which provides the meaning of life and art. It is the color of love.*

Marc Chagall

# Table of Contents

**Foreword**                                    7

Introduction                                    9

**Part One**      **Amour, Amore, It's
                  Love We Seek**

                  An Unexpected Love    15
                  Finding My Voice,
                  Allowing Love         25
                  David Elaine Story    33
                  Blind Date            39
                  Joe                   49
                  Ken and Beth          56
                  Learning the Lesson   75
                  Love Found            81
                  Murphy                91
                  My Second Love        96
                  Number 78             104
                  Saying Yes to Love    113
                  Shawn and Helen       121
                  Resonance             130

**Part Two**      **Family! Gotta Love
                  'em!**

                  Love and Laughter     136
                  A Great Teacher       149

A Tidal Wave of
Love                        155
Adopting Nicole             159
Adoption, a Love
Story                       165
Elaine                      170
Genevieve                   181
Leading with Loving
Kindness                    186
Mother and Daughter
Reunion                     194
Standing Strong             203
The Accident                211
The Heart of Love Is
Truth                       216
We've Come This
Far                         223
What Is Space?              232
The Secret                  235
I Love You, Dad             258

**Part Three**    **Tails of Love**

Wilbur                      262
Bonito                      266
Cats I Have Known           276
Cricket                     291
Cricket and Her Kids        298
Heloise, the Guide
Dog Puppy                   307

Heloise 314
Lilo, the Guide Dog
Puppy with the
Sixth Sense 321
Love between
Species 325

**Part Four** **Friends Who Touch
Our Lives and Our
Hearts Forever**

How to Say Respect
In Chinese 340
Evelyn, the Good
Mother 346
Frenchie 362
The Miracle 369
Julian 377

**Part Five** **Love, Love and
More Love**

Frances Steloff 388
French Fries 393
An "I Love You"
Lament 397
Transcendence 401
War and Love 407

# Foreword

Recently, while I rode the subway in Toronto, a gentleman dressed in clown attire came over to me and presented me with a large orange heart-shaped balloon. Whenever I travel on the subway, I constantly ask God to be with everyone on it, filling them with love and keeping them safe; from his gift, it was obvious that this man had somehow felt this love. Without saying a word, he pointed at me, pointed at the balloon, and gave me the "thumbs up" sign. Seating himself again, he kept on pointing at me, nodding, grinning and making sure people noticed–and believe me, they did.

The area of the city I live in is very culturally diverse. One can hear every language possible. With many of its inhabitants newly arrived to the country, very little English is spoken. As I walked through the area with my large and vibrant decoration, I attracted a lot of attention and excitement. People pointed, waved, jumped up and down, and made sure their friends and family saw the woman with the brilliant orange heart. Children, old men, young women– everyone responded with happiness and laughter. My smile was wider than my face! For days after, when people in the park saw me, they smiled and waved and drew hearts in the air.

Love is the universal language.

Love is what unites us in our world at a time when it seems we are too busy noticing what divides us instead. When we focus on seeing and growing the love around us, we know and share the joy that gives our lives meaning.

The stories in this book, shared from the hearts of the writers, are a gift of love and inspiration to us all. They direct us to pay attention to the many ways in which love embodies itself throughout all walks of life–from animals, to places, to people–and to see how we all are united. Love truly is "a many-splendored thing." As these stories illustrate so beautifully, there are no limits to how love can be expressed.

Compiled for all to enjoy, the stories in this book are also a gift of love from Lynda to us, the audience. They invite us to notice love wherever it is occurring in our lives and in the world around us. There is no such thing as a small loving act and when we share love with one another, we are giving and receiving the most precious gift it is possible to share.

Christine M. Harrington

# Introduction

We've all heard the saying that we are spiritual beings having a human experience. A large part of my experience has been to learn about love. Love was not expressed well in my family, and that led me to believe, as a young child, that I was unlovable. Five decades passed before I learned differently. My parents' relationship with each other left me doubting that marriage could be good, and to say that I was cynical would be an understatement. There were many hard lessons to learn as I chose relationships that mirrored and reinforced this negative view of myself. I wanted to see love and acceptance reflected back at me from the eyes of the partners I chose. Instead what I saw was what I thought I deserved–criticism, intolerance, impatience, and a real holding back of love. It seemed I was always knocking on closed doors.

For a long time I didn't live in an authentic way. Because of how I felt about myself, I played small with my life. At work, I hid. I thought that if anyone really saw me they would find reasons to criticize and reject me. I avoided participating in larger groups, fearing that they would eventually turn on me. If anyone really got to know me, I thought, they would see how unlovable I was. My inner life was very difficult, only to be magnified by my painful outer life. It was a life full of paper dragons keeping me from love, joy and a real connection with others.

In my late twenties when I was desperately unhappy in my first marriage, I found a lump in my breast. It was the first time I had seriously come up against the idea of my mortality. I thought, *I'm not ready to go now. I haven't lived life the way I want. I haven't really loved or made a difference.* That realization was the beginning of changes in me. The changes happened very slowly and over a long period of time. I received help from a therapist. Toxic relationships were no longer acceptable to me, and I moved away from them. I learned to forgive, and forgiveness allowed love to enter again. When I realized that I had let go of the burden of all the anger and blame I carried, it felt like a huge weight had lifted from me. It was very tangible; it felt almost physical. Finally, I experienced peace.

A trip to Mexico led me to the decision to put together a book of people's personal stories about the law of attraction. This decision was an impulse for me. I had no idea how I would do it or who would give me their stories, but I felt that I wouldn't have had the inspiration if things weren't going to fall into place. I believed that if I just did what was needed and stayed with it, everything would happen; the book would be published.

I started approaching people and was rather amazed at how readily they responded. Most of them were strangers or acquaintances. They put their trust in me and shared deep and vulnerable parts of themselves. I felt so honored. Their stories uplifted and inspired me when the rest of my life was going through huge change and turmoil as I adjusted to separation from my second husband. For four years I gathered these stories. While I wasn't thinking about it at the time, I can look back and realize that I was on a feeding frenzy. I was absorbing intimacy, trust, inspiration and hope. It was a very spiritual journey and, of course, it changed me. I gained confidence, made new friends and finally lost my fear of groups; instead I formed and led them. My husband and I went through a healing process that brought us back to feelings of love and deep, deep friendship. Whether our path is together or not, I believe we will always have that.

As I came to the end of the work on the *Law of Attraction* book, I knew I wanted to continue this process of gathering stories. To be able to touch people, inspire and uplift them, as I have been uplifted, and to remind us all of how connected we are, has become my life's purpose.

Deciding that the theme of this second book, *Heartbeats*, would be love in its many forms, was a natural outgrowth of my life's experience. There were many times when I had not been in my heart with others and with myself. Now, I was starting to love myself more. I wanted to learn more about love by seeing it through other people's eyes. The experience has been amazingly rich, and I see it reflected in more loving relationships. I know that by loving myself I have created that world around me.

When I considered what I meant by love for this book, I decided that I wanted it to be about love in all its forms: romantic love as in "An Unexpected Love," love of family as in "The Secret," love between animals and humans as in "Love between Species," and the love experienced between friends such as "Frenchie." I am amazed by people's generosity in sharing. I am blessed.

At this stage of the journey, I understand how simple it really is. We are either in a place of love or we're not. Everything stems from that, every response, decision and relationship. I believe it is what we're here to learn. From this place, I'm trying to live the most conscious life I can. Love isn't just something I want; it's what I am. I know that there is so much room for improvement and expansion. I welcome it with deep gratitude, a feeling of connectedness and, above all, love. I humbly share these stories with you.

# Part 1

## Amour, Amore, It's Love We Seek

# An Unexpected Love

I had been in Mexico modeling for Mexicana Airlines. At the time, my home base was Chicago and the Mexican job resulted from my being hired by a design firm who, in turn, had been hired by Mexicana to revamp their look from flight attendants' uniforms to corporate logo. At a show to introduce options by several designers to the execs at Mexicana, I presented the new attendants' uniforms with plenty of drama. The executives loved it. They made their decision based on my performance. They said that any time I wanted to return to Mexico, I could visit as their guest.

One day after my return to Chicago, I came down with a terrible cold. As I snuffled in front of the TV, an ad appeared on the screen. "Come to sunny Mexico," it said. *Ah ha!* I thought. *I wonder if they'll remember.* I called up the president of Mexicana.

"Of course," he said. "We've been waiting to hear from you."

Two days later off to the airport I went as the guest of Mexicana Airlines.

They took me down a staircase to the tarmac and had a car waiting that drove only me to the plane. It was a staircase entry, not a ramp. The other passengers, who were taken by bus to the plane stared at me and wondered who the hell I was. In Acapulco, they had someone meet me and escort me wherever I wished to go.

One night I broke away. I said I wasn't feeling well, but I lied. I didn't want this escort anymore.

While waiting for a taxi I stood on the steps of the hotel and didn't care where I went. A beautiful woman, also waiting for a cab, stood next to me. We started talking.

"Where are you going?" she asked me.

"I don't know."

"Wonderful. Come with me. I'm in real estate and I'm hosting all these people. I need a woman. It's all men."

So I went.

Throughout dinner I sat next to this very attractive young man, a pilot for Aerolinas Peruvianas. He didn't speak English and I didn't speak Spanish, but we were having a wonderful time anyway.

The next day we went to the beach where we swam and had these ridiculous drinks in pineapples. A band played and we danced in our swimsuits. I glanced around and saw a table of men who had just arrived. They all wore black socks, black shoes and white shirts with the sleeves rolled up. I noticed them, not anyone in particular, just the group of them, very briefly as they looked so out of place.

I returned to Chicago where I did a fashion show at a luncheon where the models came out and walked among the people.

"There's a man out there who thinks he knows you," the show's organizer said.

"Oh, give me a break," I said. "That's the oldest line in Christendom. I'm not coming out."

"He's with a friend of mine."

"I don't care. I'm not coming out."

She actually put our friendship on the line so I came out like a bitch on wheels. I really did not want to come out. I could not have been colder.

She introduced us. "This is Chuck Olson."

I looked at him and realized he was definitely not a masher, but a handsome well-bred man.

"You look so familiar," he said. "You have a beautiful tan. Where were you?" When I told him I had been in Acapulco his eyes shot open. "You have a black and white bikini and you are a fabulous dancer."

*Oh, my God!* I thought. He was one of the black-socked men. We sat and talked for the next few hours till they closed the restaurant.

"Are you married?" I asked.

"Well, I'm separated."

"I don't date married men. If it gets to where it's really over, then call me."

Four or five months later he called me. My first thought was *He's the nicest man I've ever met, but not my type.* We dated. I thought he was charming and we had wonderful times together.

"I feel we're going to be good friends," I said.

He said, "You and I can never be just friends," he said.

We dated for two years and we became serious. By then I really had fallen in love with him. It was the first time I had ever got to know a man and gradually fallen in love with him for all the right reasons. I admired him more and more. It was attraction and true admiration. Later we

18

discussed our first meeting and for him it was instantaneous. The moment he saw me he knew that I was the one.

We got married and were married for thirty-five of the most amazing years anyone could ever hope for. We were opposites. I like opera; he liked jazz. He liked to go to every sporting event; I wouldn't care if I never went to another one.

When we became engaged I didn't want him to buy me a ring because I had a beautiful ring of my mother's.

"What can I get you?" he asked.

"The only thing I really, really love is travel," I said.

For our first Christmas he gave me an envelope. When I opened it, I found a round-the-world plane ticket and I could go wherever I wanted.

"By the way, I'm coming too," he said.

We took six weeks and it was the most magical trip. It was just wonderful.

We absolutely adored each other. We crossed into each other's worlds. I went to sporting events with him; he went to the opera with me. I told him it was the most expensive nap anyone ever took because he would sleep through almost everything. Only when Pavarotti hit a high note did

Chuck suddenly come up and say, "Now, that's opera!" Then he'd go right back to sleep again. We melded. We had amazing times together. We'd laugh like mad. We could see the humor in situations. We went through tragedies together. We respected each other. We traveled all over the world. He was the love of my life.

One day in a fur store I saw a coat that I'd liked. We hadn't been married long and I couldn't be pushy and tell him. Instead I hinted rather strongly, but my husband never took hints.

We went down to Atlanta. Chuck was one of the Atlanta Braves' owners. We had a skybox with bleacher seats in the stands. The seventh inning stretch came around.

"Oh good, we can go and have a glass of wine or something," I said.

"No, "Chuck said. "Stay here right now."

"Why?"

"Just hang on a minute."

Then fireworks went off. The giant scoreboard carried this message.

*Happy Birthday to Cynthia Olson, wife of Atlanta Braves' owner Chuck Olson.*

As I gasped, the fur coat was draped around my shoulders. That was the kind of thing he would do. It knocked my socks off. I thought it one of the most romantic things I'd ever seen. The entire stadium sang happy birthday to me.

People use the expression of someone having your back. The loveliest thing, for me, about truly being in love is that Chuck didn't just have my back; he looked out for all of me. I knew that no matter what happened he would be there for me and vice versa. We were each other's anchors. It was the deep, deep feeling that someone just adored you to the core of your being. I'd never had that before. When we touched each other, there was an instant communication of warmth and love. It was like our souls connected whenever we touched. We loved each other, but we were in love until the day he died.

He was very strong and athletic. I know it sounds ridiculous, but I used to think *Thank God I'll never be a widow because, for sure, I will go before him.* I never expected him to be diagnosed with cancer. It was the most severe blow that I ever felt. He handled this death sentence with elegance. He never complained, never asked, "Why me?" He said he didn't want anyone to know because he didn't want to become his disease.

He was diagnosed in 1994. We still went skiing; we traveled; we went everywhere, but I could see that he wasn't as strong anymore. In 2001, after a visit with Chuck to the doctor, the latter called me and asked me to come into his office.

"Cynthia," he said. "I'm sorry to tell you that Chuck isn't going to make it."

That stunned me. I had thought we would still have two or three years.

"How long are we talking about?" I managed to ask.

"Three weeks at the most," he said. "I'm telling you now so that you can either tell him yourself tonight, or wait, and let me tell him tomorrow."

I asked to leave me alone for a bit and then said, "I think you should tell him tomorrow because he will have questions that you will need to answer."

That night was probably the hardest night of my life because Chuck sat there totally oblivious and I knew he had just a few weeks to live.

The next day the doctor told him. Chuck was very quiet, didn't break down at all, but handled the news with elegance and great dignity

Before our marriage I had led the more sophisticated life, born in England, holidaying, when I was young, in France and Italy, well-traveled. He was North Shore and hadn't traveled much. Our friends said I was the one who was teaching him. In the end I realized that he taught me an incredible depth of being, of handling things beautifully. He was totally noble.

He lasted ten days after that diagnosis. We went back and forth to the hospital.

"I don't want to die in a hospital," he said. "I want to be at home."

We had hospice care at home. If heaven has a place for saints who are not clerics or nuns, I would nominate the hospice crew who helped me look after my love during his last days. They were incredibly assuring, caring and capable....John Wayne and the cavalry in white coats.

One day one of the nurses said to me, "He's not going to make it to this evening. Talk to him."

I reminisced about all the wonderful times we'd had together, laughing about it.

"Darling, it's all right to let go," I said. "Just go. Go with the angels."

He died in my arms.

I'd always wanted to go skydiving and Chuck hadn't wanted me to. He'd said it was too dangerous. About four years after his death while visiting friends in New Zealand, I decided to do it. I have a real fear of gazing down from a height. I live in an eighth-floor apartment, and I cannot look over the terrace railing without feeling queasy.

I had a choice of 10,000 feet or 12,500 feet and I thought *I'll never do it again so I might as well go for the Full Monty*. I jumped out of the plane at 12,500 feet. The jump from that height terrified me. The skin on your face is drawn back like a bad face lift and you hurtle downwards at 120 mph. Once the chute is pulled, however, you have the feeling of going very slowly for some time and it is very peaceful and amazing. Only when the ground looks real and people don't appear like dots, do you realize that you are racing towards the ground at a very fast pace. The falling through the sky was how my life felt after his death, hurtling towards the ground, not knowing what it would all feel like, but ultimately landing on my feet. It is what he would have expected me to do.

# Finding My Voice, Allowing Love

Over a ten-year period I had relationships with four different men. None of these relationships lasted very long. Each man really pursued me and was very ardent, but very quickly the flame went out and they broke away from me as if they were dry twigs. I wondered if I was not meant to have a relationship. A long time ago I had been married. Now I lived in Los Angeles on my own.

Nine years ago a friend from my high school days whom I had lost touch with but met again by chance, called me. She asked if I remembered Bob from high school. I didn't; however, when she said she wanted to fix us up, I agreed to get together with him.

Bob arrived at my door. When I opened it I noticed that he stooped a bit. He was quite tall, handsome and in very good shape. I knew he was a bit older than I. He held a little wooden box with a bouquet of flowers and a mushy note that said *I saw these flowers and I thought they were very beautiful, and I wanted to give these beautiful flowers to you, a beautiful woman.*

I thought *he doesn't even know me,* but it turned out that when I was fifteen and we were at the same school, we had also attended the same party. He told me that when he saw me there it felt as if a light had turned on for him, and he never forgot me.

We went out for dinner. It was a lovely meal. He talked about family and even some personal issues about himself. I found the situation attractive on an energy level, although at the time, I really couldn't understand it. I didn't think we had subject matter in common. I was a teacher and a poet interested in art. He came from the banking world where he had been a president. He was a gifted mathematician– not my area of expertise, but there was something in his attention. An energy seemed to pass between us that I found quite attractive. He was very accommodating, asking me what I would like to do. I was impressed. In recent years I had only spent time with artists. I had been married to a painter. I had never been with a guy like this. He was extremely straight. He had a sense of integrity about him. It was kind of unusual after the men I'd known. He was an athlete, and overall in great shape.

We began to date and went out once a week for the following six weeks. At the end of each evening he would take me home. I didn't want him to touch me. I didn't want him to kiss me. I didn't want him to do anything that was that intimate. He would call me after the date.

"Don't you like to cuddle?" he would ask. "Don't you like to hold hands?"

"There's plenty of time," I would reply.

That was how it went. He would call me during the week. He was extremely respectful, never asking to see me at the last minute. He was kind and rather old fashioned, a guy out of the fifties, a guy who would bring you a corsage.

At the same time that I was dating him I was seeing somebody else. That relationship had all the subject matter in common, but it didn't go anywhere. I have integrity and didn't want to be with two men simultaneously.

For a couple of weeks around Easter, during the school spring break, I went to New York with a friend. While I was there I missed him. On my return to L.A. he picked me up at the airport and gave me a bouquet of flowers. He was a total romantic. I wasn't used to it. Something in that was so old-fashioned that it rankled me. On the other hand, I really appreciated it.

That night he took me out. We came back to my place and talked. I told him that I wasn't interested in any lightweight relationship. I said that I wanted a serious relationship, one of integrity; otherwise I wasn't interested at all. If he felt like-minded, then we could go to the next step. He assured me that he desired the same. I asked him if he'd care to smoke a little weed. He told me he had never done so before. He took a quick puff. I put on some music and we danced. It was the first time we made love. I had never experienced anything like it before. It was wonderful–beyond anything I had ever imagined. I wasn't quite sure what was happening.

That began our relationship.

We didn't always get along. He could not do enough for me, but I was an independent woman. He was constantly bringing me things. If he had the slightest thought that I needed an item he would get it. He was taking care of me. While I appreciated it, I felt that emotionally he was like a Tsunami. I had never had a relationship with a guy so demanding of my attention and found his actions very fifties. He couldn't get enough of me but it was too much, for me. I didn't know what to do and had to start learning how to deal with this kind of man who cared so much. I had never known a man like this.

My father had died and, following his death, my mother entered a relationship that was absolutely superb. After ten years, her boyfriend became ill and passed away. She had some business that she needed to do, and I suggested that she talk with Bob. A lawyer was taking terrible advantage of her. Bob stepped in, called another lawyer, brought my mother over there and helped save her thousands of dollars. Suddenly Bob became the person who had literally walked into the family and become "the guy," the patriarch who took care of us. My mother fell madly in love with him. He really stepped up to the plate because he loved me. This was a whole new experience for me and completely turned my head around.

Because I had ideas of my own independence and was so used to going my own way, I knew that trouble would occur here. I remember getting up in the morning and going into my own bathroom where he would never go, sitting on the pot and literally scrunching up my fists, saying, "I can't take another moment of this," because I wasn't used to that kind of return in potential. I was confronted with what came up for me emotionally. I also knew that I was honing different skills and that this man was doing something for me and my family that I couldn't do for myself. This was extraordinary. He was a real mensch through and through.

Sometimes he would call my mother and say, "Hey, good looking, how about a date? Dinner and a movie?" and they'd go out. By this time my mother had caretakers. These were significant moments. This touched me. My mother was a tough business woman. Bob diplomatically guided her in making the most ethical decisions. In the end he became her trustee. He saved her trust from some unscrupulous people.

My feelings for him began to change. *What are you doing with this man?* I'd ask myself. *This is not what you had in mind.* Over the years I began to see him differently. He wanted me to follow him, to live with him and that wasn't me. I made a bold move to Mexico. He became very unhappy and lonely with me gone. Meanwhile, I had a great time.

"Come," I said. "Be here."

At first I met a lot of resistance. But then, I wasn't forthright about my feelings.

"I found my voice, working through this," I finally said to him. "I want to be with you. I can't imagine not having you in my life. I'm not you. I don't have the same need to be with you every second."

He was off doing his own thing, but he wanted me there. It meant something.

In the beginning he wasn't very open to living in Mexico, but he tried visiting a few times. He met some people he liked and could be friends with, and he'll likely be here more often. That's where our relationship is now.

I can definitely say that I've honed my skills. There were many things about him that frustrated me and that made our relationship difficult. Instead of finding my voice and being compassionate, I would react. It was like a block of Lucite between us. I've learned to step back from what I was reacting to. I am able to see him now, from a point of compassion and care, and that has made all the difference. Underneath everything he says and does is a great deal of devotion and love. I've changed because I feel he is very special and very different from anyone I'd ever met. I wasn't sure we were that compatible because I had to find out about myself. He learned from me too. He told me once that he had learned to see his hand in things.

As a practicing Buddhist, I am learning not to focus on things I cannot change, to accept the gray areas, to be grateful for what I have. We are very devoted to one another. We speak to each other every day. I think we're together forever. I have changed in my way, but he has also changed. We're moving in the right direction together. I just want to have a good life and I think he is going to be part of it.

I learned not to be overwhelmed by him whom I once called a Tsunami because I felt that he was just rolling right over me, and I was drowning. As soon as I found my voice, all of a sudden I realized I could simply say what I wanted and he would respond. I was just who I was. I was free to love him.

# David Elaine Story

*David and Elaine West, Sausalito,*
*California*
*Born 1951 & 1952 respectively*
*No. of Marriages: two each*
*Years together: 15*
*Years married: 12*
*Years on each other's radar screen: 23*

Our story begins in 1987, when Elaine comes to work as a graphic designer for the California State Compensation Insurance Fund. This state agency, headquartered in San Francisco, California, provides workers' compensation in the competitive insurance market. An ex-colleague of hers, Judith Singer, has recently come from another agency to work in the Communications department as a writer. Subsequently, she entices Elaine to seek an inter-department transfer which would have them teamed up once again to produce publications.

An early project for Elaine is to lay out the newsletter for the National Association of State Funds. As she reviews a stack of photos to go in the newsletter she wryly comments to Judith that all the photos seem to be of the stereotypical insurance-man: pasty-faced, over-weight, middle-aged white guys. But she finds one that doesn't quite meet that description.

"Great name – Dave West," Elaine says, as she checks out the photo caption.

"He works for us," Judith replies. "In fact, he works on this floor."

What a coincidence, Elaine thinks. There must be twenty guys in this stack of photos from all over North America, and the only cute one works just down the hall.

"He's married." Judith says.

This last detail squelches further inquiry.

Flash forward several months. A graphic design request of David's lands on Elaine's desk, so she drops by to discuss it. Several things happen in that encounter: David immediately notices Elaine's beauty and charming personality. Elaine inquires about David's sailing posters and comments on her general, and her brother's specific, love of sailing. After a relaxed conversation about same, social radar screens flicker brightly, and an extremely boring design project is set on its way to completion.

Flash forward another seven years to 1994. After occasional casual contact in the hall, the radar screens have gone dim. David is now managing a department in another building across town, and Judith is one of his best and favorite direct reports. But there's trouble in his life: he is splitting up with his wife of ten years. Realizing he's out of sorts at work, he decides to tell his direct reports what's going on to free them to work around his distractedness. A few months later Judith attends a typically challenging, rewarding and fun meeting in David's office. On her way out, she stops at the door.

"I have two words for you," she says. "Elaine Zapf," then exits.

Cupid has launched an arrow, and one radar screen flickers back to life.

It's now early 1995. Along with nearly 400 other people, David and Elaine are both at an annual corporate party in San Diego honoring the company's best and brightest. While they may qualify under those criteria, David and Elaine are not present on merit. Elaine's department puts on the event and uses its staff to support it; David is there as an annual attendee and a senior manager. On the last evening, a live band performs and the dancing runs late into the night. David screws up his courage and invites Elaine to dance, and she graciously accepts. Except for David's few obligatory dances with his female staff attendees, Elaine and David dance the night away. At the end of the evening, David asks if he can call for a date when they are back at work, but adds that he is traveling for the next week or two so he will be in touch after that.

Each of them is pleased at this start, but only one of them acts on it – Elaine. She is spending a few days in town with her mom and a brother who works as a spectator boat's commentator at America's Cup yacht race. Elaine invests $2 in a souvenir of the event for David.

Nearly a month passes. Elaine wonders why David hasn't called. She decides to send him the America's Cup souvenir in the inter-office mail on a Monday morning with a mildly caustic note (that, happily, gets delayed). That very evening, just hours *before* that note and souvenir would reach his IN basket, and after unexplainable, but not uncommon, procrastination, David picks up the phone and calls Elaine. He's cut it *really* close –

calling just one day later would've appeared forced or disingenuous. Fortunately, it is a well-known fact that inter-office mail NEVER moves between offices, even in the same city, on the same day, so it is clear David acts of his own volition. They make a date for that Friday evening. The next day the souvenir arrives and, reading the note, David breathes a huge sigh of relief for having made the call in time. Catastrophe averted.

The date goes swimmingly. The radar screens burn blindingly. True, unwavering love blossoms.

Two years later David and Elaine are camping out for a weekend sailing event for David's class of small (18 foot) sailboats on a glorious mountain lake in the Sierras. The couple has set out for a romantic sail on an unseasonably cool and misty day in the early evening. David has smuggled aboard a bottle of champagne, one broken and one unbroken acrylic champagne flute and an engagement ring, all bought clandestinely for the occasion. Huddled in their foul-weather gear, sitting together along the side deck as they sail slowly up the lake, David asks Elaine to be his wife and the long-time, happily single bachelorette joyfully says, "Yes." The ring is donned and the champagne consumed as the last remaining wind of the day dies. Elaine responds as any good First Mate, but not as all new fiancées would – she paddles the last quarter mile to the mooring. At the helm, David pinches himself. Who could ask for more?

A year later (1998), David and Elaine marry in San Diego in a small, intimate wedding. Today, they still pinch themselves.

# Blind Date

The phone rang and I heard a gorgeous voice! The voice was low, rich, very sexy and belonged to Bob–my blind date–someone I had never seen or talked to before and who was also in the same boat. What must he be thinking of my voice? Too high? Too old? Too young? Blind dates are much too stressful. Why did I ever consent to one? My previous and only blind date had turned into a relationship lasting, off and on, for more than five years. I didn't know if I wanted to go through that again. My heart had been broken the first time. So, when I had recently seen my girlfriend, Telly, and she asked if I was seeing anyone and I answered, "No," I knew something was up.

My mother had just had a serious cancer operation and I had moved back home with my parents to help, as I was the only single one left in my family. I had broken up with my last boyfriend after a couple of years and thought I would take some time for myself. When Telly asked me if I would double date with her and her boyfriend and his best friend, I said,

"Maybe." She considered that as a "Yes," so she had given my number to this fellow, Bob, who was on the phone NOW!

We started to talk and discovered we had a lot in common: cottages, music and books. I found him easy to talk to so I relaxed and enjoyed the conversation. I learned he had started his own business a few years before. He also had a small jazz group and they played now and then at various places. That sounded really interesting. We both decided that we would prefer to meet each other alone without Telly and Bob's friend, in case things did not work out. Our first and maybe only date would be the next Thursday, June 11, 1959. As we both liked jazz, we would go to the Plaza Room to hear a group and get to know each other. It sounded like a good plan and he would pick me up at 6:30 p.m.

This phone call came Sunday, so I thought about our meeting quite often during work, when out in the evenings and on the phone with my girlfriend. Finally, after a very busy four days at work, Thursday arrived. My girlfriend dropped in after work and we decided she would stay with me for moral support until my date appeared. When she asked me what Bob and I planned to do and I told her, she freaked out!

"Do you know what day today is?" she asked.

As I was so busy at work and thinking about my date I really did not know what she meant

"Today is elections day," she said. "Didn't you vote? Did you forget that the bars will be closed?"

"Oh no!" I said. "The Plaza Room will not be serving and will be closed."

I sank down on the chesterfield and just looked at her.

"What are we going to do?" I asked.

Needless to say, an anxious discussion took place and it was decided we would suggest a movie. Great, but I did not have a newspaper so did not know what was playing. (You can tell this was not the age of the Internet.) At this point a knock sounded at the door.

Bob had arrived and right on time. What should I do?

I opened the door tentatively. Luck was with me. Before me stood a vision. The man was a six foot dream. He wore a cotton black, grey-and-white striped shirt with a mandarin collar, (no tie, great), charcoal sports jacket, grey slacks and he looked so cooooool. I was very impressed. And his voice was so smooth.

I invited him in and we introduced ourselves. There was a moment of silence as we surveyed each other and then we both spoke at once. We decided to go to a movie and get a newspaper at the corner.

I suggested we could leave now and, on the way, drop my friend at the subway.

"Sure," Bob said.

As we left, my friend whispered, "If you don't want to see him again, let me know."

We decided on *Captain's Paradise* with Alec Guinness and Yvonne De Carlo at the Hyland. The movie started at 7:30 p.m. so we hurried along. He had his own car, a Ford Meteor. It was so pleasant not to have to take public transport.

The theatre was crowded, but we found good seats and settled in to watch the movie. Bob remained quiet during the movie but I felt comfortable beside him and enjoyed the movie which was a comedy about a ferry captain with his route back and forth between Gibraltar and Morocco. In his cabin he had a picture of his wife in Gibraltar and halfway across to Morocco he would push a button and the picture would switch to a picture of his wife in Morocco. Needless to say, you can guess what happened. His Gibraltar wife decided to surprise him in Morocco and discovered the other wife. Then both wives worked out how to surprise and punish him. It was a good movie and really broke any ice Bob and I might have had. There was no problem with communication between us; actually it was very enjoyable.

After the movie we went next door to a restaurant, The Tops, for something to eat. After all our talking and the movie I was really hungry. I ordered a Western on brown and Bob ordered a Clubhouse. I had no idea what a Clubhouse sandwich was, but did not want to let on. When the food arrived Bob's sandwich looked fabulous. I had a section of it and ever since then I absolutely love Clubhouse sandwiches. To this day, whenever I have one, I get a warm feeling.

We returned to my apartment around 11 p.m. and Bob said "Goodnight." He had to be up and at his store for 8 a.m. He owned a paint and wallpaper decorating store in East York which he had started when he was only twenty years old. Being a small business owner impressed me, and later I would discover, required much hard work and many long hours.

We said goodnight with a light kiss and off he went with the line, "I'll call you."

"Please do," I replied and went up to the apartment.

I wondered if I would hear from him. I hoped so, as I really wanted to see him again. I think he awakened in me the feeling of maybe we could have some great times together. Over the past year I had been fairly cautious and felt unsure if I wanted another relationship. I had almost decided to skip getting attached and stick to dating with nothing serious, but Bob made me feel I wanted to see him often.

The next day was busy at work and then I headed up to my parents' Muskoka cottage for the weekend. I brought along two friends from England who lived in our apartment building to show them our cottage country. It was a good weekend and we had a great time, but I kept thinking of my past Thursday and wondered if I would receive a phone call. We arrived back in Toronto after supper on Sunday and he called. Bob wanted to see me again and that was the beginning of a relationship that has lasted for the next fifty-two plus years.

How could a blind date last that long? Magic. Bob and I became inseparable. That year 1959 was a great year. We went to the cottage, listened to jazz, danced at Bigwin Inn, and I just knew we were a couple. During the July 1 weekend up at my parents' cottage we both knew it. In September Bob took me fishing. Not just fishing from a dock or a boat on a lake, but real fishing! Bob went to a lodge near Barry's Bay so he knew the people who ran it as well as the guides. We were going for a few days. Bob arranged for separate cabins and because it was the end of the season with few guests, we were treated as one of the family. Each day Bob and I woke up early and headed out to fish at a different lake. To get to most of the lakes required walking some distance, more than just a few yards. The one I remember the most was Echo Lake. We only walked a couple of miles but it seemed like a hundred. When we arrived at the lake, the boat waiting for us was not only padlocked, but an old skiff. It belonged to one of the guides and Bob had the key. We got in and off we went. It was one of the most beautiful lakes I have ever traveled on and it was absolutely quiet except for the odd bird. You could not hear any traffic, cars, trains or airplanes. Even the water seemed quiet and we felt as if we were absolutely alone in the world. What a feeling, so awesome that I can't really describe it! We caught a few bass and then had to trek out in near darkness to the car and back to the lodge. The weather was not great; it rained and even snowed a bit. I was so tired I could barely eat my supper and can't remember falling into bed. This was only one of the days of fishing; I believed that Bob was testing me to see if I could survive. As a matter of fact, I really enjoyed those days which substantiated the feelings I had for Bob whom I wanted to be with forever.

By Thanksgiving we knew we would get married. I had mentioned to Bob that I would like him to speak to my father. I had promised Dad that if and when I ever decided to get married, I would have my intended speak to him first as a courtesy. This proved more difficult than we expected. Mom and I sat on the front lawn at the cottage and my father was bringing the boat into the boathouse after having had a ride. Bob popped down to the boathouse to speak to Dad. It was like watching a Laurel and Hardy movie. Dad went in and out one door of the boathouse while Bob went in and out the other door. I am sure Dad did it on purpose, but I never got him to admit it. Mom and I giggled as she knew what was going on. Then Bob cornered Dad inside the boathouse and they stayed there for quite a long time. I asked Mom if maybe Dad had jumped in the boat to leave. Finally, Bob and Dad came out of the boathouse. Dad had his arm around Bob. Dad approached us.

"Mother, meet your future son-in-law," he said, and gave me a hug and kiss.

Bob looked embarrassed but he held up well. We had taken the first step.

My birthday was at the end of November and it was also Grey Cup Football day, November 30. Bob gave me my ring for our official engagement. The ring was set in white gold and centered with a gorgeous brilliant diamond surrounded by a tapered baguette diamond on each side. We had an engagement/Grey Cup party with about twenty friends and we announced our wedding date. It would be June 11, 1960 – exactly one year from the day we met.

Needless to say, the year flew by, and after some lovely showers and dinners, our day arrived. We were married in the new beautiful Trinity College Chapel at the University of Toronto, and my oldest brother, a priest, married us. My other two brothers were ushers. My father walked down the aisle with me and my mother cried. I had my four best friends as my bridesmaids and matron of honour. I had always wanted to go to Niagara Falls and we did so for our first night. Even if it was a corny idea, it was lovely as Niagara Falls is wonderful at any time.

Bob and I have had more than fifty years together and many ups and downs. We never thought we would make our fiftieth but the years passed very quickly, especially the last twenty. We have two gorgeous children, Laura and Ward, and three lovely grandchildren.

We basically have good health and are still happy together; we look forward to many more years. We live with the goal of enjoying every minute of every day of every year as you can't ever go back, but you can always go forward. Love is precious and must be renewed and protected over the years. As some old adages go, "You only get what you give or you only reap what you sow."

God Bless.

# Joe

I think that the best part of my life was my most unexpected meeting with an ensign in the United States Naval Reserve during World War II. At twenty-three, I was on the executive training squad at R.H. Macy Department Store on 34th St. in New York City. One evening, as I was about to leave work, Betty, who had a locker next to mine, turned to me.

"Are you married?" she asked.

"No, I'm not," I said.

She then proceeded to tell me about her wonderful son who was in the naval reserve. His ship was coming into New York, Brooklyn Navy Yard just after completing the Murmansk run, a difficult trip. Betty and her husband had arranged to have dinner with him that evening. Wouldn't it be nice if there were four of us? It might be pleasant if he had a date, she mused. I thought this strange because they hadn't had a chance to see him. Rather than bringing a perfect stranger with them wouldn't they rather have had him to themselves?

It was the middle of the week and I did not have a date. Had it been the weekend I certainly would have. However, I hesitated.

"He's a Phi Beta Kappa, top of his class at Dartmouth," Betty said.

*Well,* I thought, *he's not stupid so at least we'll have a good conversation going.*

"All right; I'll go," I said.

As luck would have it, she cancelled and said I'd have to meet him on my own, a blind date. She told me where he would meet me after I finished work. Because it was wartime, there were so many men in uniform meeting their wives and dates. He was the last one there and I decided it must be him.

"Are you Joe?" I asked.

"Yes," he said.

"I'm Ann," I said. "I'm your date."

Well, that was it. We had the best time. He was terribly attractive, and I think that men tend to come across even better in uniform. I thought he looked wonderful. We spent the whole evening talking. We just talked and talked and talked. To this day I have no idea what we talked about. He had five days left of his leave.

"Can I see you again," he asked.

"Yes."

"Tomorrow?"

I already had a date, but I said, "Oh yes!"

I broke all the dates because this man seemed so special to me. Tremendous warmth came out of him. He had a very kind face, a giving face. It was magnetic. Sparks flew immediately. Living in New York I had dated enough men to know a keeper, someone special when he appeared on the scene. I knew right away he was for me, and so did Joe. It was fate, destiny, whatever you want to call it, we agreed. Five straight days of seeing him made me realize that this was it.

For nine months I waited for him to return from the war. He did, in July, 1946. He was an aide to Admiral Kincaid of the Seventh Fleet. Joe was an operations officer, which meant he took huge maps of the oceans and all the ships in that fleet and moved those ships around into the positions required to go into battle. He became a great favorite of Admiral Kincaid. I hadn't realized until much later what that job entailed. I didn't understand until many

51

years after that Joe was just a master of challenges; he really loved them.

I had a career as a buyer, which was very exciting and which I loved very much indeed. It never occurred to me that I wouldn't leave it to help him and follow wherever he went, which was to graduate school at Harvard. We moved to Cambridge, Massachusetts. The G.I Bill gave Joe $80 a month so I supported him through college. We stayed there for the next eight years.

After graduate school, Joe was asked to go on faculty as a Junior Teaching Fellow. Then he became an Assistant Professor and then an Associate Professor. Those were wonderful years. I found them terribly exciting. At first I was really undone because, unlike everyone else, I didn't have an advanced degree. I had such reverence for them. I thought *How am I going to deal with these people with their degrees and I won't have anything?* I was rather worried about it. After my first few faculty parties, I thought, *Forget it. I don't have to worry about a damn thing. These people have feet of clay.*

The years in Cambridge were so interesting. Henry Kissinger was in our group. George Bundy who became Secretary of State and Arthur Schlesinger were there.

We met so many fascinating people, each one with an ego as big as a globe.

We were asked to live in one of the undergraduate houses because the system is based on the Oxford University system. Each house has 350 to 400 boys. The Senior Tutor resides there with his wife, and the couple, along with the Assistant Tutor, run the house and take care of all the problems. We, with our two adopted sons, lived with these boys and I was their crying pillow.

After Harvard we went to Wesleyan in Middletown, Connecticut, where Joe taught. As much as we loved Cambridge, he would be stuck for years before a career opening came up if we stayed. At Wesleyan, Joe became the Provost, which meant that if the President couldn't do his duties, Joe would take over.

After thirteen years at Wesleyan, Joe was offered the position of President at Skidmore College in Saratoga Springs, New York. By virtue of the job, we suddenly found ourselves on all kinds of invitation lists. Nelson Rockefeller had us to his Fifth Avenue apartment for dinner. He gave a party for the astronauts after their first flight to the moon. I sat next to Neil Armstrong who was shy and self-effacing. We got invited to the White House for a luncheon with Jimmy Carter. We also attended a dinner there with Lyndon Johnson. Joe and I were in a receiving line which was not supposed to stop, but the person in front of me started talking to Lady Bird. So there I was, standing in front of Lyndon Johnson who towered above me. He asked me some polite questions and then there was this big pause. His budget had just come out.

"Mr. President," I said. "I have just looked over your budget."

"Oh, and what did you think of it?" he asked.

"You're spending too much money," I answered.

I felt like a fool, but Lyndon Johnson just laughed.

At home, Joe was terribly kind, undemanding and appreciative. He was so challenged and so focussed on his job. He wasn't able to spend as much time with our sons as he should have. I tried to make up for it. I didn't resent it because I knew the job was demanding, and it was important that he did it. I honestly think that Joe could never have done it without me and he did say that. I knew that we would never part and that I would always be by his side. As a team, we really made a great contribution. Without him I would not have developed into the person I became, and without me he would not have turned into the man he was because we were so intertwined. I loved him right through until he died. We were together for forty-three years.

## Ken and Beth
## Synergy

We are soul mates from past lives
Meeting and completing in the now
The best of me, I am with him
I am the best that he is too
Split apart we've come together
We can just be
He him I me
And revel in loves' synergy

- Gail B. Murray

Sometimes destiny lands us in a place we hadn't planned. The year 1979 turned out that way and if I could relive one year of my life, that year would be it.

How I came to be at the cast party for *One Flew over the Cuckoo's Nest* wasn't the only serendipitous happening that summer. Bill, the director for this Scarborough Theatre Guild production had insisted I was perfect for the part of Sandy. I hadn't auditioned, but as the Guild's membership secretary I had been merely helping him with readings at the play's auditions. Bill had previously rung an emotional soliloquy out of me as Juliet in *Romeo and Juliet*, and I trusted his assessment.

So here I was at lead actor, David's house, with Jean Serge my flamboyant actor-businessman boyfriend who had come down from Ottawa for the performance. We'd been dating for five months but our relationship was winding down. Jean Serge spent most of the party downstairs socializing. I hadn't made it past the kitchen talking to dark-haired Italian Mike, a fellow teacher and friend of David's.

"Before you go, I'd like to introduce you to my pal, Ken," Mike said.

We walked around the corner into the living room. Ken was tall, slim, wearing jeans and a red kangaroo jacket. When Mike called his name and Ken turned to face me, I was taken by his huge blue eyes and the long sweep of sandy hair across his forehead. He had an amazing smile and exuded charm.

I felt I was living a pivotal moment like in *West Side Story* when Tony sees

57

Maria across a crowded dance floor for the first time or when Romeo is smitten the minute he spies Juliet at a party. I couldn't take my eyes off him. We were so instantly drawn to each other. When he asked for my number ten minutes later, I didn't hesitate to pass him a pen. He wrote it on a piece of toilet paper.

David phoned a few days later.

"Will you give Ken a call?" he said. "He's the squash buddy of mine that you met at the party. He keeps phoning me. He's lost your number three times."

I was flattered by his persistence and ignored his inability to follow through, a trait that caused him to lose job after job.

I called him.

"Can I come over tonight and play my guitar for you?" he asked.

"Yes," I replied without hesitation.

Both Ken and Mike showed up. Mike had the car.

I overheard them arguing on my balcony.

"Why don't you take off and leave us some space," I overheard Ken say on my balcony.

"But I met her first at the party." Mike said.

"Have you seen how she looks into my eyes?" Ken asked. "She likes me."

So Mike gave me up to his best friend.

Ken played his guitar for me and I was his.

Sometimes I think it's about timing. Ken and I met at the right time in our lives. I was twenty-nine to his twenty-six. My teaching career was well established and I'd performed in live theatre for the past five years. I was a petite blue-eyed blond with shoulder-length hair. I'd dated a slew of handsome, non-committal men in my twenties, and I was minutes from turning thirty. And I was very confident.

Ken had tasted despair. After partying away his first year at Queens, he failed his courses. He slit his wrists and spent six months in a psychiatric hospital. The doctors diagnosed him as mildly schizophrenic. When I met him he was in remission. His medication was working and so was he. He told me this on our second date. I had taken psychology at university and felt I could handle his illness.

During those first few heady weeks we were inseparable. It didn't matter what we did as long as we were together. We were soul mates from past lives meeting and joining together in the present.

He was simply the most romantic man I had ever met. My handsome young Adonis had charm in spades and a wild sense of humor. He had a riotous combination of flirting and teasing. He called me "Murray" and referred to himself as "Fenn." He introduced me to artists Jackson Browne, Neil Young, James Taylor and played the tunes of my favorite singer songwriters–Bob Dylan and Simon and Garfunkel. When he performed his own lyrics they resonated with me, especially the September one, because as a teacher September meant returning to reality.

September's here again my friend
Heart on the mend
World without end
Amen.


I recall sitting adoringly at his feet at our parties. A cigarette hung from his guitar fret as he sang, surrounded by candlelight and my friends sipping wine or herbal tea.

In those first months he gave me an antique silver brooch, taught me squash (skillfully placing the ball on my racquet) and invited me to the courts to watch him in action. Ken worked as a squash professional and had matches with clients at posh clubs all over the city. At the refined Donalda Club we enjoyed champagne brunch after his games.

Ken's father was vice president of a successful international company and had memberships in both the Granite and Cricket Club. One Sunday, Ken in his grey suit and I in my ice cream dress, pale blue with a strawberry and vanilla belt, brunched at the prestigious Toronto Cricket Club. I felt like an English trifle– something highly prized and sought after. That day he bought me a single red rose and signed his father's name to the chit. He used charm and style to his advantage. He had class, came from money, but had little of his own. He was used to the high life of private schools and upper middle-class clubs. This was new to me. I was drawn by the elan but repelled by the phoniness I encountered at the cricket matches and cocktail parties.

*That first year everything was touched in beauty. I finally understood the phrase to see the world through rose-colored glasses.*

Ken was a tender, attentive lover. He made love to me with more than his lithe, young athletic body. He made love to me with his voice, his music, and his gossamer words. I think he and Keats would have been good mates. He never rushed me but covered me in kisses. He verbalized his love sometimes in a hushed whisper, other times as a statement with a rakish wink and smile. We were always touching, holding hands, cuddling, both in public and in private. Love wasn't something we could hide or deny.

We would lie in an embrace and gaze into each other's eyes. I loved how our bodies melted into each other so effortlessly. One night when he entered me and was about to climax he whispered, "It's like coming home."

There is no question he was my soul mate. We were like the Aristophanes' story about the split-aparts finding each other and becoming whole. He unleashed that part of me that is lighter than air and lives on dreams, who like Keats and Shelley is on a quest for love and beauty. I can freeze-frame those water-colored moments even now, like the lovers on the Grecian urn.

We wrote music together and engaged in soulful late night talks. One of the most romantic things he ever did was read Tolkien's *Hobbit* aloud to me in bed as he held me in his arms. Our love lived on so many levels.

Another romantic gesture was the love song he wrote for me that June entitled *Apricot Rose*. In the song he described me as "a little bluebird that I once knew."

I taped his song and rushed to school early the next morning to play it for my teacher pals who were in awe of our fanciful relationship.


**Apricot Rose**

I met a girl named Apricot Rose
Got soft blue eyes and a cute little nose
She wears a smile like nobody knows
But oh how I know Apricot Rose
She never gives an excuse to be sad
Her lips taste sweet
It's so hard to get mad
Like a little bluebird that I once had
She lingers on my mind and I'm so glad.
(Verse One)

OOOO OOOO Apricot Rose
You really got me going. Oh how it goes
I keep on wondering as it grows
Why you took a man like me, Apricot Rose. (Chorus)

Late at night she whispers in my ear

"It must be hard to find a treasure so
rare"
Little Girl I love you whenever you're
near
Give me a reason, my heart's up for
treason
And if I was teasing I wouldn't care.
(Verse Two)


When I met Ken he was living in
Rosedale in an old house converted to
shared accommodation units. Most nights
we spent at my apartment, but this night it
was late and we were downtown at Doobies
so decided to stay at his place. It was my
first and last visit there. I think most of the
renters were young men who merely slept
there because the place was unkempt. We
had to sidestep the garbage in the hallway.
His room was large and decorated in early
Salvation Army chic and the metal coils
from the mattress were starting to dig into
my back. We stopped our lovemaking to flip
the mattress.

Without a car, he often missed the
last bus so slept over most nights at my
apartment. He was seldom at his place. We
didn't put much thought into moving in
together. One day we picked up his clothes
and records and he started paying me what

he had given his landlord. The disparity in our incomes wasn't an issue for me as long as he made some contribution. At that time, not too many couples chose to live together openly. I don't remember we ever talked about getting married. We had both survived traumatic divorces. We were in love. We didn't need a social and legal contract. We just needed to be together. Would I finally achieve my dream – someone who loved me for myself and whom I could share my life with as an equal partner?

Today, years later I feel validated when I read Elizabeth Gilbert's views of balancing the separate and the together in *Committed*. Gilbert refers to it as a wifeless and husbandless marriage with no role identification and no giving up personal dreams.

That first summer together we frolicked in the lake at the Outlet in Sandbanks Provincial Park. He'd pick me up and swirl me about in the waves. We played like children. After a few days of sleeping in separate rooms while visiting my parents, we ached to be together. Now I'd simply rent a bed and breakfast. I wasn't so confident then to stand up to my strict mother. Ken had a friend, Jake, in Belleville so it seemed a good pretense. We drove the half hour to Belleville and the old pals caught up on each other's news. Then we were offered the couch. Some friend! Later my free-spirited sister chastised me.

"You didn't tell them you're living together!" she said.

Even if we had told them it would have felt strange to make love in your parents' home.

Ask me to describe a perfect day and it would be a hot August afternoon. Ken and I dined at Fenton's Garden Room beside a small birch tree decorated with glittering lights. This elegant bistro with fresh bouquets of freesia and classical music in the bathrooms, served only the finest French cuisine. Later we arrived at the red velvet Royal Alex Theatre to experience *A Chorus Line*. As an actress I strongly identified with this show and grueling auditions so I imagined myself out there on the stage with the actors. Each character revealed their heartache and dreams as they tried out. Being a part-time actress and performing filled a need for me. It opened up a rich inner life and reawakened my creative self after a harrowing divorce.

Where else could I go to the prom in a pale blue organza dress *(Grease)*, play a tart and party at a mental ward *(Cuckoos'*

*Nest*), dance salsa in a nightclub in Havana (*Guys and Dolls*) or be a young American princess falling in love with a Russian (*Romanoff and Juliet*), all safely and vicariously not as me, but as the character; then go to work the next morning and teach nine-year-olds Canadian history?

This love of the arts, especially of musical theatre, was something that Ken and I shared with a passion. My alter-ego experienced full rein in the spring of 1980 when Ken and I performed together in Scarborough Music Theatre's *Camelot*.

I had persuaded Ken to audition with me. With his rich tenor voice, he sang Lancelot's signature piece, *If Ever I Would Leave You*. Add to that his boyish charm and good looks and he was in. The musical score, however, was difficult and they were only casting six women as ladies of the chorus. The director didn't cast me; instead he offered met the position of Assistant Stage Manager, working alongside him taking blocking notes. I learned a huge amount about directing which I later put to use staging school musicals, which furthered my career. It also gave me time to spend with my sweetheart as rehearsals were four times a week.

Two days before opening night, one of the ladies of the court sprained her ankle and could only hobble about in a cast. This threw off the dance numbers. The director came to me.

"Beth, could you do me a big favor?" he asked. "I remember that you danced in *Guys and Dolls*. Would you take on Barb's part?"

Would I? Was this where the term break-a-leg originated? Wardrobe fitted me for the costume and the cast devoted an entire night to all the dance numbers. The May Dance was exhilarating as the knights lifted the ladies and passed them around, and then swung in a huge circular motion of interlocking arms. Every night we tested our daisies and hair pieces before going onstage. I performed with my sweetheart and showed despair as my knight, Sir Lionel, was injured in The Joust. Backstage, the cast awaited the final curtain as Arthur and Guinevere enacted the poignant closing scene. We ~~misted up before bursting~~ on stage to a

[1] Last lines sung by Arthur in *Camelot* by Alan Jay Lerner (play and lyrics) and Frederick Loewe (music). The original production played on Broadway in 1960, won four Tony Awards and ran for 873 performances.

curtain call of standing ovations. The lines continued to echo in memory:

"Don't let it be forgot that once there was a spot

For one brief shining moment that was known as Camelot."[1]

Ken and I shared this rich theatrical experience for twelve glorious shows. Again If felt that timing and destiny were at play in my life

Our first Christmas together was idyllic. His parents bought a real tree. Ken and I sipped chardonnay and danced to Harry Belafonte as we strung silver tinsel. When Belafonte sang "Daylight come and me want to go home," it was my turn to think I had arrived home. Ken gave me a delicate gold ring with a tiny center diamond,

"For love and friendship," he said.

Today it sleeps in my musical jewel box.

On Valentine's Day, 1980, Ken sent me a singing telegram–a gorilla gram– delivered in clear pitch by a large man dressed in a gorilla suit. My grade five students pointed and laughed non-stop. They delighted in seeing their teacher blush in embarrassment. I became the talk of the school.

Of course I kept that telegram sung to the tune *Baby Face*

Ma cherie, I'm up in heaven near you, ma cherie

My poor heart is thumping, you sure have started something

Valentine, whisper in my ear that you'll always be mine

I didn't need a shove, cause I fell in love

With my poopsie sweetie pie.

One night at Doobies over juicy burgers, we talked about travel. I'd been teaching about British Columbia and had fallen in love with the idea of Vancouver's mountains, ocean and old growth forests.

"My cousin Nick lives out there; maybe we could visit him," he said.

"Have you been there?" I asked.

"No, but I'd like to go. I'll call him."

We flew out in July and Nick and Ann put us up on their pull-out couch except for the first few days when they were on holidays. Then we stayed at the charming ivy- covered Park Royal Hotel.

For breakfast we had carrot and orange muffins, fresh squeezed orange juice served in crystal goblets, and of course, Earl Grey tea. With his upbringing this was the norm for Ken, but a special treat for me.

Travel enriched our relationship. Ken was easy, laidback, and eager to do anything I suggested. I was the planner; he injected the fun into our ascent of Grouse Mountain; we wobbled on the swinging bridge at Capilano and looked up old pal Pip from their cricket tour of London. Pip and his fiancé invited us to Granville Island for a live production of *Pippin*–a soft rock opera. Ken imitated Gene Kelly as we skipped and tap danced our way down Gastown's cobblestones in a light drizzle. Just when I figured it couldn't get any better, Ken suggested we cycle the sea wall at Stanley Park–tandem. Our bodies moved effortlessly in bed; could we maneuver a tandem bike? Not to worry, my guitar-playing songwriter had been the Junior Squash Champion at eighteen and his athletic skills remained intact.

Ken could appreciate beauty which we explored in abundance at Butchart Gardens. We drove across Vancouver Island to Pacific Rim National Park. I plunged into the waves and couldn't feel my feet, numb from the icy Pacific. Later we splashed in the surf. We were at our best as carefree playmates. Ever the romantic, Ken found a large stick and carved *Ken loves Beth* in the sand.

We felt the ancient primal energy of the Douglas firs at Cathedral Grove. The mountains were never far from sight and the entire experience became part of our internal landscape. I remembered that the nineteenth century romantic poets were inspired by nature. To share this level of travel with someone you love was beyond words. Ken, however, found the words and sang them to me:

> Mesmerized by the love in your eyes
> And the stars upon the hills
> The mountains far away they cast their spell
> We go on impulse through the night
> The shadows flee before dawn's light
> The secret of the world comes to my sight

After an incredible two years our relationship started to unravel slowly, a thread at a time. No death or drastic ending like star-crossed lovers of history or literature, just a slow realization of the depth of his mental illness and a final acceptance of his doctor's diagnosis at the Clark Institute that our relationship was not viable.

Collin's English Dictionary describes romance as "an intense love affair with scenes remote from ordinary life." The Oxford Dictionary describes a romantic as "a person who is highly imaginative and emotional and concerned with ideals rather than reality." This aptly describes Ken.

As carefree lovers, we had suspended the real world, created our own reality, made fantasy real. My personality could manage duality. His could not. I could straddle both worlds. He could not. I could balance a demanding career with romantic adventure. For the longest time, I believed in and supported his potential but could not motivate him to fulfill it or make hard and fast career choices. He appealed to my sensibilities, but could not sublimate his music the way I could my acting, to search out suitable and satisfying employment.

Can romance survive daily challenges or is it a tenuous and fleeting thing?

Keats could have worked as an apothecary but chose to devote his life to his art and died tragically at twenty-three. Even the finest champagne exposed to the air goes flat. I had sipped its sweet nectar.

Perhaps romance has an expiry date. Not all relationships are meant to last. Some teach us and help us grow. I had been the leading lady of my own very real fairytale. How many women long for that heightened sense of life? Perhaps the current phenomenal success of the *Twilight* Saga is symbolic of our need for high romance.

I often see my Ken in the tender young lovers on the screen – Noah in *The Notebook* and Edward in *Twilight*.

In The *Twilight* Saga, Bella has to die to consummate her love with her vampire lover. My heart gravitated to an Edward but my instinct for survival won out. To live day-to-day, I needed a Jacob, someone who is warm, loving and grounded.

I will never forget that magical time – a time shared with Ken.

© 2011 Gail M. Murray. Used with permission of author. Gail Murray is a freelance writer based in Toronto. Her poems have been published in Canadian Authors Association Toronto Branch's *Wordscape* and Ontario Poetry Society's *Arborealis*. Creative non-fiction and travel pieces have appeared in *The Globe and Mail*, *Trellis* and *NOW Magazine*.

## Learning the Lesson

At six years old I started school. It was the first time away from home without someone going with me or holding my hand.

My dad saw me crying.

"What's wrong, Mary?" he asked.

"I'm afraid," I said.

He grabbed my hand and said, "You don't have to be afraid. You are never alone. If you want to be successful in school today there's only one thing you have to do."

"What's that, Dad?"

"You just have to show love to everyone you meet," he answered.

I looked at him. "What does that mean?"

"Well, you see, you're holding my hand," he said. "That's showing love. By giving someone a smile and always being kind you're showing love. You do that to your classmates, to you teacher and everyone you come in contact with, you'll have a beautiful day. You'll love school and they'll love you."

He made me feel that it would be easy and I couldn't wait to get to school.

At school, I immediately started to show that type of love to everyone, smiling, holding hands, telling girls I liked their dress, telling the teacher I was happy to be there. I remember that she had beautiful eyes. My dad always complimented me about my eyes so I told her she had pretty eyes. It worked like magic. I loved being in school and each day when I woke up I couldn't wait to get there.

One day out in the playground, this girl came up to me and pushed me down. She was very mean to me. I thought, *Oh no; it's not working!* I went home crying and told my dad.

"Dad, it just doesn't work all the time," I said.

"I still promise you that love always works," he said. "I tell you what you do. When you go back tomorrow, go up to this little girl at playground time and tell her you forgive her for pushing you down and being mean to you and that you still love her anyway."

When I considered this I thought, *Wow, I don't know if I can do that.*

The next day I went up to her and I told her that I loved her and that I forgave her. She was so stunned she just stood there and stared at me. Then she came over and held my hand. That moment showed me love is more powerful than anything else. From that time on, throughout our school years, we were the closest of friends. I heard her tell that story to almost any new person we met, when they asked why we had such a great friendship.

She has since passed away, but this story remains in my heart now and forever because I do know that love is the most powerful energy in the world, and it has worked for me my whole life. It has opened doors in everything that I tried to do. I was successful in all my careers. For me, love is not something you think about on a daily basis, but it creates your soul and your heart. It becomes the substance of who you are. The magic of it all for me is that I didn't realize how other people recognized this love until I was older and started receiving feedback from people who asked me how I learned to show love.

I also asked the people who helped me why they had promoted me and been there for me and it always came back to love.

"The way you were with people, showing love to everyone, we always knew that you were going to excel," they said.

Because I have been so successful all through my career life, I wanted to give back, to be able to show love to people who have less than I do. This lifelong passion led me to San Miguel de Allende, Mexico. I wanted to experience another culture where I could uplift people who are the poorest of the poor.

While I was in San Miguel, a man from the United States came there part-time. While in San Miguel he helped with his charities. He approached me and asked me if he could help me with my charities. He saw me with the American doctors who helped the special needs children that I volunteered with. He saw my dedication and wanted to find out about me and get to know me. For a year and a half when he came down all we talked about was charity and giving. We couldn't understand how everyone didn't do what we did. We shared ideas about improving our respective charities. He already worked on an international basis with charitable organizations. He recognized my talent and passion for showing love and giving and asked if I would like to do it on an international basis. I was overwhelmed. I had not thought that far. So many times in my life I hadn't thought about the future. I just went through doors as they opened and magic happened. He was a man who could and did help materially and gave of himself on an international basis. He wanted a partner to help him with this. I flew to New York to meet all the people he worked with and I loved everything they did.

He invited me to go with this charity to the second poorest place in the world, Burkina Faso in West Africa. We had a very rough journey through the desert, working with the poorest of the poor. We stayed in primitive places with few comforts, and we really got to see each other from many angles.

At the end of the trip he looked at me and said, "You are so liveable. You are the same no matter what the situation is. You are always showing love and uplifting people no matter what."

This partnership led to another type of love, the male and the female. I had always felt that my life was like a piece of cake, and it was wonderful cake that I always had, but this added the icing. To have that icing on my cake is to be able to travel the world and to uplift the poorest women in the world who make less than a dollar a day.

We work with and contribute to charities out of New York. We travel with them on a worldwide basis. We contribute to them generously, but we also give of ourselves and go into the poorest countries in the world, offering loans and giving donations. We teach people how to earn more money and, ultimately, offer education, which is the key.

For me to have met a partner who has the same heart that I do, who wants to give love and help people, is magic. We are able to share our thoughts, lives and travel. We have it all, the passion and love. It's as if I have finally, through my journey with love, found ultimate love. I can't imagine there being anything better than what I have now.

# Love Found

I'm Laura and six months ago I came to San Miguel de Allende from the United States. My move has been much more than I could have imagined, partly because I met someone special down here. The beginnings of my journey started a year or so ago, when I had a slight stroke caused by stress, partly from dealing with a son who has significant health issues. I also realized that despite having friends in my hometown of Washington, D.C., life there was too complicated and busy for me to receive the emotional support that I needed. You could say that one of the reasons I had a stroke was my life lacked love–an oversimplification but not incorrect.

A friend of mine who had introduced me to San Miguel four years ago suggested that I consider it in my wish to relocate away from Washington. The more I considered this idea, the more I thought, *It makes sense.* There was the favorable exchange rate between dollars and pesos. However, the compelling reason was that during my brief visit down here I had seen more happiness and joy among people with less material goods than people I had seen in Washington. In San Miguel families cherish everyone–little children, grandparents, parents. Their way of life might not be that efficient by U.S. standards, but it seemed a more complete way of living that really celebrated life and I felt drawn to that.

This past year has been about packing up my home, getting ready, saying goodbye, at least *hasta luego*, to my friends and family in Washington and the actual trip down in late August accompanied by one of my sisters. My family had doubts about my capability to make such a gargantuan change of moving to a foreign country whose language I didn't know. I was grateful for my sister's support.

I needed to find a place to live, and that is the beginning of my story. In San Miguel no two places are even vaguely alike. When you search for a place to live, you need to look at every single apartment or casita that might be available. You find out mainly by word of mouth. I located a place to stash my stuff, but it wasn't great and I quickly realized that I would never be able to make it my home. I began my effort to find somewhere else to live.

However, I needed to learn the language and so that was also a priority when I arrived in San Miguel. Every day I left my place and walked to my Spanish class. This happened to be the street that my now friend, Johnny, walked down in the opposite direction while heading from his home under renovation to his apartment. He's a friendly guy so when we passed each other he introduced himself, as did I.

Weeks later as my quest to find a place that really felt like home intensified, I ran into him again and yet again.

"If you know of a place, please let me know," I said to him.

He gave me good ideas which I followed up on.

Lo and behold, a couple of nights later, Johnny knocked on my door and asked me if I'd like to join him for shrimp cocktails. I said, "Yes," because I'm a friendly person too, and I thought that this would be fun. We moved from having shrimp cocktails to going around the corner for dinner, to his asking if I'd like to see his house which was at the end stages of renovation. I said, "Yes," and it was great. We saw each other the next day and I think there's hardly been a day since when we haven't seen each other.

Let me tell you about Johnny. He is seventy-one years old and tall, 6'0". I'm fifty-nine and short, 5'2". He's big and handsome with a white beard. People say he reminds them of Ernest Hemmingway. His faith means a lot to him and he has a wonderful childlike quality. Because he is an artist, he has the ability to express this quality. He makes playful Christmas ornaments, such as a star or a mouse out of bits of wire. He cuts animal coasters out of leather– an elephant, a crocodile and other wonderful animal likenesses. John is very smart, curious, and funny.

He finds real joy in children, and he's very proud of his two grandsons. He's devoted to his family and his friends and spends time keeping in touch with them. These qualities drew me to him because what I needed at this time in my life was somebody with the same values as mine. Family and friends are very important to me. Johnny really cares about my children because he really cares about me. My son, who is twenty-two, has been diagnosed as

bipolar and he is also ADHD. He has
significant problems in trying to grow up
and is not there yet. Currently he lives at a
facility in the United States. I would have
thought that my son would be a non-starter
for a relationship with most men because he
does need my love and attention. John has
given me some of the best advice I've ever
received from anybody regarding my
relationship with my children.

"Just be his mom," he says. "Call
him frequently. Tell him you love him, and
listen to what he tells you. You don't have to
say anything."

My daughter has had to live
independently for so long because of my
preoccupation with my son.

"Send her something every week
even if it's little, even if it's just a piece of
your hair," Johnny says. "Just send her
something and let her know that you love
her every week."

That means an awful lot to me. He's
helping me be the person that I want to be
and that's big.

We are different in that not only is he
eleven years older than I am, but he was
born into a life of privilege in New York
City and I was not. Every evening, he would
sit down with his whole family– mother,

father, and brother to dine. They had three desserts to choose from and three bottles of wine. I am one of five children of a mother who, essentially, raised us alone. I come from Irish Italian immigrants so our evenings were much more carefree and free-for-all. My family's meals did have their own ritual of sitting down at a properly set table and saying prayers before we ate. However, unlike his family table, ours contained no silver.

Because Johnny lived the life of private schools and an Ivy League university I appreciate his ability to step away from it. He told me that people in his social sphere when he was younger were not necessarily nice, and he didn't want to be that way. People were so aware of everyone else's lineage. It was hard to get away from that set social structure. He wanted to be human, to give.

After college, he chose to go on to the Harvard Theological Seminary to learn more about religion and its underpinnings. He didn't want to take the easy answers of catechism, but to understand more. He was a social worker for ten years and lived with those men who were in such dire straits that they were given a place to live for a while so that they could get themselves back on track.

He chose to live in an environment of physical deprivation. He really was committed to helping these men do better. His sense of service to others means a lot to me.

He's a very gentle lover. He's very conscious that physical intimacy is part and parcel of communication and that you don't go to bed with someone just to fill your needs. It is the most intimate form of communication. I've never had any man so attentive to what I feel, what I think, what works for me, and what doesn't work for me. At the same time, he tells me what is good or not good for him. The exploration of physical intimacy has been a heck of an education for me.

This home that he's making is beautiful. Although furnished in a style that is not familiar to me I am impressed by it, but wouldn't decorate my home in the same way.

The story of us as a couple is really the journey for me having lived most of my life alone despite having been married. My husband and I had separated for ten years, gotten back together and then separated again, partly due to the challenges of our son's mental problems and partly due to our own incompatibility. Because of this, there are innate assumptions I have made about my life that I get up in the morning and plan my day. It is an evolving process that I check in with John to see how "us" may affect "me" as I organize my day. Early in our relationship I sat down one morning with my cup of coffee without thinking about offering a cup to him. Johnny gently pointed this out. It underscored how long it had been since I had thought about anyone else. He said that love is really a verb, not a noun. That helped me a lot in thinking about the right thing to do. I believe it will take a long time for me to feel settled enough in our relationship without pausing to think how my plans impact him.

When I came down to San Miguel it was to start a new life and, hopefully, find someone that I could build a relationship with, but given the percentages of about sixteen women to every man, I didn't hold out much hope. Johnny had ended a relationship that had been quite emotionally traumatic and was interested in having a fulfilling relationship in his life. For me, it was a little soon. I hadn't even found my physical home yet. I was trying to find my way, trying to get settled, find my friends, learn the language and locate basic necessities such as food. It was almost as if

Johnny got plunked down into my life too soon, and I wasn't quite ready. But because of his sympathy and interest in me, I didn't want to push him away by saying, "It's not convenient right now to have a relationship."

So we have begun to see each other almost every day. How do you love someone when you're in mid-life and you haven't really done it much before? It has been a very conscious decision, on my part, to choose to love him. I recognize in that option, that I choose what I infer about his motives around certain behaviors of his. He's not perfect. Who might be perfect for me? Maybe it's somebody, like me, who enjoys watching the Super Bowl or just hanging out at a bar because it's such a nice camaraderie at times, but that's not him at all. It is my decision in what light I want to see him and that's been very illuminating for me. On the other hand, it won't do if in loving someone else I lose myself in the process. I am figuring out what is essential to me to be true to myself. He would be very happy if I spent a lot of time, quietly, with him. For me that wouldn't work. I'm too new here, too curious and active. I want to explore this place fully. We have had our differences about how much time we're actually present to each other. It hasn't been completely easy. Each time our intense discussions about this have left us closer than before. The walls are coming down.

At this moment I'm hopeful. I'm particularly aware that loving someone else is a process, not the goal. It is something that happens every day with no assumptions about the outcome. Not only is he good enough, but this is such a great opportunity for me to just play this out, in other words just use *love* as a verb. For me to truly love him I have to give it my best shot and accept that it may not work. Whatever it is that we have, in the meantime I want it to be truly loving.

# Murphy

When I was a fifteen-year-old high school student in Long Beach, California I had a boyfriend. Then I met his friend, Dick Murphy. I broke up with my boyfriend and started dating another boy, Steve, who was also friends with Dick Murphy. The four of us– Steve, Murphy, our friend, Richardson and I would go to Salt Beach to surf. These three fellows attended university. Murphy was a tall, blue-eyed, dimpled surfer. He was gorgeous. He was scary sexy. All the girls adored him. Murphy and I always laughed and stared at each other. Sometimes I watched him surf instead of my boyfriend. I always had a huge crush on Murphy, but I never said anything about it.

Steve was my high school sweetheart, and I went with him for four years. We married and stayed together for four more years before we broke up. Although we all lived in the same town, I lost touch with Richardson and Murphy until twenty-five years later when they landed on my doorstep.

"We've had a huge crush on you for twenty-five years," they said.

I thought they were just whistling Dixie. I didn't see either of them after that day for another twenty-five years.

I'm sixty-five now, and a few months ago I was on my Facebook page when I saw a picture of Murphy there as a friend of a friend I might want to be friends with. In the picture, Murphy wore a big diving mask. He had a camera and held a big eel in front of him. I befriended him on Facebook. He wrote back asking, *Is this the Sylvia of Richardson's and my fantasies?* Yes! I was surprised that he even remembered that he had said he had a crush on me.

We started emailing immediately. He's a published author and a great writer. What he wrote to me is pure treasure. The emails are the most romantic. I do not know how the man keeps going. He is one of the world's top marine biologists and sometimes he gets scientific/romantic.

He has his PhD in marine ecology. Since1968 he worked with the late Jacques Cousteau. Murphy is an international speaker and is incredibly bright and fascinating.

After two months of emails we fell in love. During this period we wrote maybe five or six hundred email letters to each other. At one point he suggested that I might like to join him. He designs programs to help people appreciate warm tropical waters for one of the top hotel chains. He wanted to meet me in Puerto Rico or the Amazon rain forest in Brazil.

I wrote *Come to San Miguel,* and he came. I didn't have any doubt about how I felt about him. I knew it was going to be absolutely incredible. When he arrived he stepped out of the taxi and looked at me.

"Is that my princess?" he asked.

When he came through the gate I saw my prince and I ran to him.

We walked around town. He met my friends and was so gracious. I'm proud of him. Our time together was so passionate, so magical. He gave me his book on coral reefs and the day after he left I sat down to read it. I thought *anyone this bright could not possibly love me.* I started getting really insecure. I emailed him, *You're gone and now I can't believe it.* He wrote back *I want you and need you. We will be together as soon as it's possible.* He's never lied. He asked, and with my permission, he shares our letters with Richardson.

We decided to meet about four times each year. We do not talk about getting married. We don't discuss me going to Santa Cruz to live with him or his coming here. I think, for me, it's just right; it's perfect. It's as magical as it gets. I don't think I want any more. I am not very possessive. We send each other ten to twenty email letters a day. In one of his letters he wrote that he always felt that he had missed out on the adventure that is Sylvia because I was first friends with Johnny Caldwell. Then I dated Steve Blackburn. Richardson and I were always friends. At that time, I didn't want to be around Murphy because he was too cute. I didn't want to get myself into any emotional trouble. He was a ladies' man. That has never appealed to me, but at this point I thank every girl he ever practised on because now he is perfect and I know he's mine. He thinks of me as a pristine goddess and keeps saying, "You're so pretty." He's my silver-tongued devil.

Every Christmas, Richardson and Murphy stay at Steve Blackburn's house. Each time they kayak through the canals at Long Beach, and they talk about me. They have done this for forty years. Murphy is still somewhat astonished that our relationship is so incredible. It is the best relationship of our whole lives, and I am very happy.

# My Second Love

I was in my sixties. I was a divorced woman and had been on my own for almost thirty years and had two wonderful children. The marriage busted up when they were four and six. At the time I thought, *Well, that didn't work out too well. I don't think I'll be doing that again.* So I got on with my life. I had a good career as a social worker and enjoyed being single. There were lots of dates, lots of experiences and I traveled. In short, I had a wonderful life, or so I thought.

About a year or so after my retirement I went to Cape Cod to help my sister move into a house that she and her husband had just built. It was in Chatham, a place I had never visited. Before I left home I had my investment club meeting at my house in Baltimore. During the evening I mentioned my upcoming trip to Chatham,

"Oh, Chatham, I know this wonderful man there," one of my club friends said. "He's been so bereft over the death of his wife. She died a couple of years ago, and you really would like him. You should call him."

As my friends knew, I really didn't like being fixed up that much. I had plenty of dates and plenty of alone time too. I had never met anybody during the past thirty years that made me want to marry again. I still wasn't very open to getting married.

You really would like him," my friend said.

"I'm not going to marry some guy whose wife died," I responded.

My friend made sure that at the end of the meeting she was the last one out the door.

"Now listen, I put his name and address in your purse," she said. "I don't care if you go see him or not, but you could at least give it to your sister. She's new there. He's old, old time Chatham. He knows all the people that she might need to know, like the right plumbers, electricians, etc.

"Yah, yah, Okay, thanks," I said.

Off I went to Chatham to help my sister. After three days of doing nothing but moving furniture into her house I'd had enough. I love my sister, but I was so bored. I thought, *I've got the name of that guy in my purse. I'll just call him and get out of here.* I called him and explained who I was.

"You're welcome to come over, if you'd like," he said very politely.

I raced right over there. He'd already gotten out the cheese and crackers. We sat in the backyard. He had a beautiful home on the water. It was a wonderful sunny June day. I thought, *We don't know a thing about each other. What the heck are we going to talk about?*

"Where do you live in Baltimore," he asked.

I told him,

"I know it well," he said. "I grew up in Baltimore."

All of a sudden we had a connection. We knew the same people and had almost the same circle of friends. A real conversation started and we didn't stop talking for the next couple of hours.

I could tell he was a very cultured, rather shy academic. He had attended Princeton and got his PhD at Yale. He was an oceanographer, a scientist type. I'm totally not a scientist type. It's all literary for me, so it was an odd mix, but there was an attraction there. He was different from many of the guys I had dated who were suave and egotistical– more interested in how they

98

came across than in me. This man had a sense of self that was strong but not the least bit egotistical. I sensed that he probably didn't know women very well either. He had married a girl from Nantucket after they had been friends for a long time, so he didn't have any experience with women like I'd had with men. Their marriage was happy until her death, and he was still in a sort of mourning period when I met him. However, I could see that he was ready to get out of it.

We decided that we would have dinner the next night, and we saw each other a few more times. I returned to Baltimore and we started corresponding. I think we really fell in love over email. We emailed each other all the time. We started this long-distance romance, and it was so exciting. We decided that as we wanted to know each other better, we would travel together. We were both retired so this was easy. He came to Baltimore. I went with him to Oregon where he lived half the year. We went on trips to Egypt, Anguilla and the Galapagos. I'll tell you, traveling together really lets you know about people. That's when stresses happen and people can't be on their best behavior all the time. This was a man that I had feelings for and those feelings kept growing and growing.

His lack of experience with women had me a bit worried. I could tell that he was a marrying man. This relationship was turning somewhat serious but I, as a social worker, had counseled a million couples in love and saw what happened later! As a divorcee, I was very cynical about how things can change in a relationship. I decided that he needed to know himself better in relationship to women. He had had this wonderful wife and not all women were like her. He was serious in his commitment to me.

"No, you need to go and date people and find out about yourself in relationship to women," I said.

At first he resisted this suggestion, but then he got interested in it because I made the idea sound so intriguing.

"How are you going to go about doing this?" he asked. "How are you going to find these women? I'm certainly not one to go into a bar and pick somebody up."

"Well, there's this dating site on the Internet called The Right Stuff. It's for people who have attended all the Ivy League schools plus the University of Chicago, the University of Virginia and, I think, Stanford."

He got on the computer in my house. I helped him put his profile up on the site. He received many hits. Women were very much interested in him. According to them, he had all the right stuff. He's also a good-looking man. He made dates with women from Washington and Philadelphia and used my house as the base.

While I pushed this dating-other-women, I have to admit I was getting a little jealous even though I didn't show it. When he returned home, I needed to hear all about his experiences. He didn't find anybody on the east coast, but he also looked when he was in Oregon. He didn't ask any of the women out; they always asked him.

At this point, I visited him in Oregon. Through the University of Oregon, we took a trip down to Baja on a research vessel to whale watch. Along the way to the ship, during our drive down, I would be in our hotel and he would be on a date. When we boarded our ship, I found that our room was the size of a closet with bunk beds for very small people, one small mirror and a tiny bathroom down a very narrow hallway. I'd brought all my makeup and my hair stuff. I could see that this wasn't going to work. I put all my makeup and hair stuff under the bed, so this was the real me. This wasn't the glamorous me anymore. Of course, everybody else was in the same situation, and we had a great time. He had wonderful friends, a lot of them scientists. It was one of the best trips we had.

Well, it finally came to a point; after one of his dates he came back and asked, "Could we stop this now? I've dated sixteen people. Could you just come to the Cape this summer, live with me and let's see how it goes."

"Yes," I said, and fortunately I was in a position to do that.

Now it was a question of getting married. I still argued about that.

"Why not just live together?" I asked. "What's the matter with that? We'll just be partners. We'll travel and it will be just like we're married."

He was just old-fashioned enough to say, "I don't want to call someone my girlfriend at this age."

At that time I was sixty-two and he was seventy.

"That kind of makes sense," I said.

"I just want to be married. I want a wife. I don't want just a girlfriend."

So we planned our wedding.

Eight years have passed. We've had a very happy marriage. We still don't have the common interest of science, but we have other common interests. His family and mine have blended beautifully. Between us we have seven grandchildren. It's a good life.

No matter how single or alone you are, there's always somebody out there. He might just be around the corner. You just have to take those chances.

# Number 78

Love has taken many forms in my life. I had a loving father who named me Minerva for the goddess of wisdom. He loved me so much that he wanted me to be that goddess. He taught me about Martin Buber when I was eight years old and Emanuel Kant when I was eleven. He gave me five dollars for every A that I obtained, so I got all A's. I entered Smith College on a scholarship. Daddy really set me up for success. I suspect that everyone who is successful has had a parent like that.

My mother was a simple woman who grew up on a farm in Russia. She sewed my clothes and loved anything soft or living such as pets and food in its preparation stages. My parents were the ones who taught me early in life about love, devotion and caring.

I grew up in Washington, D.C. As a teenager I was very popular, greatly romantic and had many boyfriends. Almost every night I would go to dances at various hotels. I felt happy in my adolescent years.

At the age of twenty-two, right after I graduated from college, I married a prince. He had all the right credentials: Dartmouth and Harvard Law School. Although I'm an intelligent woman, I sank into the 1950s and the feminine mystic. Man and wife were considered one and he was my one. I loved him very deeply and as his wife, I depended on him. Unfortunately, after a dozen years of marriage he became ill and almost died. He had to stop smoking, and he started drinking. He turned into an alcoholic and died in the streets at fifty-two.

For the next ten years I dated several very strange men. I could not believe that God had created such men. Then I got engaged to a very distinguished man who was chief economist at the Federal Reserve. Before we could marry, he died of a brain tumor.

I felt a little like Typhoid Mary, and I was afraid of marrying anyone for fear they would die. My first requirement in a partner was somebody healthy who was going to live. Also, I wanted a man who could make me laugh.

At this point, I had obtained a doctorate and operated a writing consulting business. I taught at the University of Connecticut and began to evolve as a writer. In 1998, I decided that I really just wanted to find someone to travel with. I was tired of the whole romantic shebang – searching for another prince and believing that I would find a soul mate. I had evolved consciously through many spiritual and New Age workshops.

I was successful in most of the things that I undertook, but I wasted much energy looking for someone ideal. So in 1998 I said to myself, "Why not just find a good friend that I can travel with?" Because I have always been oriented towards males, I decided I had enough women friends and didn't want any more. Then I did something rather startling to most people. I decided to write a book about men over sixty and what they wanted. I understood younger men and their desires, but I didn't understand the strange men I'd been dating. I decided to do some research.

I obtained one hundred profiles from three dating services: The Right Stuff, for people who went to good colleges, which I did; Single Travel Companions, and Single Book Lovers. Like Scheherazade, every night I would interview a man. My TV sound bite, later, was. "I did a man a night." Obviously I meant interviews. The men lived all over the country, and the long-distance interviews, four or five hours, in some cases, were expensive. I wanted to do this right and really get a sense of who they were and what they wanted. Most of them talked to me and, I believe, rather honestly.

It took a year from the start of this interview process to compile the book. There was an incredible amount of data. I decided to structure the book on *The Canterbury Tales*. I was Mrs. Chaucer and these men were on a pilgrimage looking for love, not for God, and they would tell me their stories. I picked twenty-nine of the best stories; many of them were funny.

A friend pointed out that I had found types. True, but I also considered them as individuals. In the process I met Jack Calkins. He was interview number 78. Jack lived in Washington, D.C. and was looking for someone to travel to the Easter Islands with him. I didn't want to go there, but we talked for five hours. He had a deep voice which I found very soothing. He was a politician. My husband had been a politician. My husband and Jack knew the same man, Ken Mansfield, a friend of ours living in Washington. Ken was the Inspector General of the Department of Energy. When I learned that Jack knew Ken I realized that Jack was not an axe murderer, so I felt safe when he asked me if I would meet him. This was in April 1998.

Several of the men I had interviewed wanted to meet me but I didn't have the same desire. I preferred caution, which women need to exercise under these circumstances.

Jack traveled a lot and so did I; therefore we didn't meet until August. He drove up to Hartford, Connecticut, where I lived, and came for dinner. By then, we knew each other through letters and phone calls. I felt safe because of his friendship with Ken. It was not love at first sight, but Jack is intelligent. We had a wonderful conversation at dinner. While I did the dishes, he put a CD on and whirled me, dancing, around the room. I'd known him for two hours. All my life I had loved to dance, and I had never had a man who was a great dancer; Jack was. That started things off. We began meeting each other on weekends.

On one of the weekends we drove to Cape Cod where I have a summer place in Truro. We went to Provincetown to dinner at my favorite restaurant, The Martin House. I love the restaurant and we bopped around the town afterwards. In a shop I picked up a pheasant boa, put it around my neck and started prancing around the store. When I looked at the price tag and saw $350. I put it down because it was outrageously expensive.

A short time later I went to a wedding in California and, when I returned home I found the boa in a long skinny box outside my door. Attached to it was a note reading, *To keep you warm until I see you again.* How romantic! That started a new level of interest in me.

Although he was a politician, Jack loved to read the great classics – Hemmingway and F. Scott Fitzgerald. I found when I dated all those odd men that many didn't read. I'm a great reader, and it's wonderful to be in this same room reading away together.

He is an Episcopalian and I am Jewish. He is a Republican – a middle-of-the-road Republican, a Rockefeller Republican, and I am a Democrat. He had worked in the White House as Chief Advisor to President Ford, and Ford was an okay man so our politics didn't make our connection impossible.

In December we went to Anguilla in the Caribbean and had a wonderful time. By then, I was in love and in a romantic relationship with him. I was not dependent on him because both of us had our own means. We decided we would be equals sharing everything fifty-fifty.

We looked at our wish lists and found that San Miguel de Allende was at the top of both our lists, so we traveled there. We both fell in love with it. We bought a house together and we're ecstatic here. We love this town. Everything about it is to be loved – the colors, the sunlight, the people, the food and the friendships.

Friendship has become the most important thing in my life. Jack and I have known each other for twelve years. I think we are deep friends. He's eighty-four; I'm seventy-seven. One trait I love about Jack is his *joie de vivre*. He gives himself five or six birthday parties every five or six years. When he was seventy-five he had six birthday parties, the last one in Venice. When he turns eighty-five we'll have the first birthday party in San Miguel with seventy or eighty people who have become our friends since we came here. We like each other's friends. We have harmony.

I love Jack for his quiet intelligence. He's so alive. He's attractive in a very distinguished-looking way.

I also love Jack because he is a wonderful host. I'm kind of a hostess-with-the-mostest myself. As a politician's wife I threw good parties, but now I have a fantastic cook who prepares amazing meals and even does the shopping. It is the best life I've ever had.

I love that Jack appreciates me. He loves me to write. I didn't have that kind of support before and it's wonderful to have it now.

I love his dry sense of humor. There is nothing ostentatious about him. He loves theatre. He loves art and collects it.

He has faults, but we are both mature enough to recognize that everybody does. I love that he will admit that he's wrong. That is a rare trait in a man. If I point out to him that my feelings are hurt or that he has done something obnoxious, he will always say, "I will try to do better," and my anger dissipates. He doesn't always succeed, but he does try.

Now we have an ideal relationship. We're together in San Miguel for three months. We're together at the Cape in June. We travel in August, back to San Miguel or to Edinborough, to the Fringe Festival. We spend time in Naples, Florida. During other parts of the year we live separately. We have time off. He is more vigorous than I with a greater desire to travel and he often travels on his own.

Our life would not be ideal for many people because I am happy with him and I love him, but I'm also happy without him. I require that space. I am a writer and have to be alone a lot. I don't think our situation works for everyone because many women want to be dependent and have a man in their lives all the time. I've learned to appreciate what I have now. I used to be dependent and I know what that feels like. I find that knowledge freeing.

When I counsel women on how to find the right man, I try to discover what they really want. Have they ever considered the various kinds of love: sexual love which dies when you are much, much older, the huggable and comforting love, the friendship love, the deep, deep attachment, the agape love, the love that comes when you think of the other person first. Jack and I have had all of them. I feel very fortunate that I found him.

Minerva Nieditz

# Saying *Yes* to Love

Throughout so much of my life, I have heard and read that God is Love. It seems that I have been saying *yes* to Love throughout the second half of my life.

As a young man with a wife and children, I was busy pursuing my life and career – the nicer car and the bigger house. My career took me to senior positions in such large corporations as General Electric and NASDAQ. In those endeavors, I learned that satisfaction from material things was short-lived. A very painful divorce turned my life upside down, and I moved from Chicago to Phoenix for an executive position at a large corporation. That was the first half of my life–and the beginning of the second half.

I briefly left my two children, ages three and six, in Chicago, but the opportunity soon arrived for my boys to join me in Phoenix. That was a moment of decision for me. I knew that in order to be a full-time, single father, I would need to make drastic changes in my day-to-day life.

I would have less time to spend with my friends because I would need to be home more and be responsible for my sons' young lives, their schoolwork, medical care, drive them around, get them involved in sports and take them backpacking and mountain climbing. I would have to cook and grocery shop. I said *yes* to what I now know was the call of Love to give in ways I had never given before, and to receive an opportunity to bond with my children. Some of the more mundane domestic duties were harder and many other things were fun. I found it difficult to cope with a few of their life issues, but we (including our Siamese cat) all came through in good shape. The best words I ever heard from my sons were "I love you, Dad."

The boys saw me as a father, but I needed also to nurture them as a mother would. I took Tommi and Matt to see the movie, *Mr. Mom,* where a father takes on the day-to-day responsibility of caring for his children–in both serious and humorous ways.

"So that's the way it is with us, huh Dad?" they asked me later at dinner.

"Yes," I said. "That is the way it is!"

It was around this time that an awareness of my inner spiritual nature began to emerge. I did some serious seeking that went beyond the books about spirituality I had been reading. Sampling, seeking and learning, I started going to different churches, temples, and ashrams. At the time of my divorce, I was particularly moved at a retreat hosted by the Franciscan Fathers in Phoenix. Thanks to my Catholic background, I bore the guilt of divorce. When one of the young Franciscans let me know it was okay to be divorced (and to remarry), I was forever freed of an enormous emotional prison. All I could say was, "Thank you, Father!"

I started to define the difference between spirituality and religion. For me, religion had become dogma with restricting borders and absolute obedience. Spirituality kept showing up in uplifting, positive, freeing, guiltless ways. It produced positive changes in me and the way I viewed everything. I no longer saw myself as a victim of circumstances, but as a spiritual being with a Divine connection that gave me all the love, wisdom and power I needed to live a more positive, creative life in service to others. No shame, no blame. What a gift!

Spirituality became Love–Love in action.

My friends noticed a huge, positive difference in me.

"What happened?" they asked.

I could not quite articulate it then the way that I would today, but I know that Love was at work in me. My growth was unfolding at a much-accelerated rate. I was saying *yes* to Love.

After my divorce, I dated a number of different women, but I did not want to remarry until the kids were on their own. As that time approached, I did become open to meeting someone special and remarrying. For some reason, I had a notion that I would meet a woman with blonde hair who came from a different country.

One day, I spoke at a conference at the University of Phoenix. During my presentation, a lovely woman in attendance asked me an extremely intelligent question. She asked me how I was able to complete a university degree as a single, working adult with two kids and an executive level job requiring plenty of travel. I responded that I was extremely good at time management, patience and loved to cook!

I thought, *This lady is very bright.*

A social hour followed my talk. Love was at work again as we gravitated toward each other and began a conversation. She had a gentle and sweet way about her.

"I appreciated your question," I said.

"Well, thank you for your answer."

"Where are you from?"

"Canada," this lovely woman with blonde hair replied. Her name was Wendy.

Again, I said *yes* to Love. Wendy and I dated for a couple of years. We decided to marry and settled in California while Wendy completed a Ph.D. in adult education at the University of Southern California.

Within a year of our marriage, Wendy was due for a routine medical checkup and sought out a doctor where we lived. Wendy's doctor examined her and took her history.

"Oh, by the way," the doctor said. "You need to have a mammogram."

Wendy was thirty-nine at the time.

"Why?" she asked. "Breast cancer does not run in my family. I exercise. I eat right. I live a good life."

"Because if you want to be my patient you must do so," the doctor said.

Wendy had the mammogram, which surprisingly revealed a small tumor. Hearing the diagnosis of breast cancer was shocking, but because of early detection, it had not spread. The removal of the tumor was successful.

I prayed for Wendy, affirming the complete goodness of Love, and Wendy did heal. I surrendered our concern to Love, and then let it go. It was a spiritual experience beyond description. It was a wonderful way to say *yes* to Love.

Wendy's first cancer was a warning that cancer was possible. Her second occurrence of breast cancer came ten years later. That was alarming. Another routine examination had discovered yet another tumor, but this time the circumstances were tougher, resulting in a mastectomy, plus the removal of a number of her lymph nodes.

The blessing was another early detection of this cancer. Nevertheless, now our situation was both physically and emotionally devastating. I spent an extraordinary amount of time caring for Wendy, as well as dealing with my work and many household duties. We became concerned with the financial impacts, the fact that Wendy was in the midst of her doctoral program and had to put a one-year hold on it, and the perennial question of whether or not her cancer would be cured then–always an after concern. Sadness, anxiety, doubt, and anger were the emotional buzzards that kept circling.

Wendy and I again prayed and she experienced another physical healing. There also were emotional, mental, and spiritual healings because the floodgates of Love were wide open for both of us. We were increasingly saying *yes* to Love.

I became more loving and accepting of others and myself. I became more forgiving and more centered in Love. I was able to start making a change from being ego-driven to accepting whatever Love offered. I could relate to other people more easily. My work became more purposeful and meaningful. Life became increasingly effortless. My attachment to material things lessened. Money now continued to show up, but not something that I sought as an end, but rather as another gift of saying *yes* to Love.

A few years later, I had the opportunity to interview for the role of president of Unity, a non-profit spiritual organization that supports over three-million people of all faiths worldwide. However, we would have to move from our home in southern California to Kansas City, Missouri. Wendy was resisting the possibility of this move. When we visited

119

Unity's headquarters during my interview there, Wendy stepped out of our car onto their grounds and turned to me with a smile,

"If they ask you to take the position, you have to say *yes*!" she said.

They did ask and one more time I said *yes* to Love, because I felt that serving as president of the organization was mine to do at that stage of my spiritual development. Serving others is a gift that I have been blessed to receive.

We left Kansas City four years ago and we continue to say *yes* to Love in service to our world–me as an author*  and speaker about the power of our spiritual nature in work and business, and Wendy as a professor of adult education at the master's and doctoral levels.

Saying *yes* to Love is our way of life for good!

*God Goes to Work*, by Tom Zender, John Wiley & Sons, 2010, www.tomzender.com

*365 Meditations at Work: Inspiration on the Job*, by Tom Zender, 2011.

# Shawn and Helen: a Love Story

Shawn and I met in April 1984.We worked at the Madison Avenue Pub in Toronto–he as a dishwasher and I as a busgirl. Shawn was seventeen and I was sixteen. Both of us already lived on our own and dated others. We hit it off right away – not romantically on my part: it was more in a good friend kind of way.

We talked in the morning as I prepared the Pub for lunch service. Between his kitchen duties he helped me. While we worked, we chatted about our relationships, our families and our worries about such concerns as paying rent and other bills. I found him easy to talk to. I think being on our own at such a young age drew us together. We were kindred spirits.

At the time, I had no idea that Shawn actually worked evenings and not days like me. The poor guy did double shifts, one, not his schedule, without pay, so he could hang out and talk with me. I didn't discover this until many years later, when he finally confessed.

Shawn didn't tell me right away how he felt because he figured I had enough on my plate with my not-so-nice boyfriend. However, Shawn did confide his feelings about me to one person, Dennis, his friend and mentor. Dennis gave him what turned out to be good advice.

"Be patient," he said. "If it is meant to be it will be."

Shawn is an extremely patient guy.

About a year later, Shawn and I started dating. Approximately a month afterwards, we moved in together. It didn't seem too fast for this young and naïve couple. At first, all went well. We started spending time together with our families. We spent Thanksgiving at his dad's place and Christmas at my sister's house. We slept over there Christmas Eve so we could wake up first thing in the morning with the kids. It turned into a real family affair. I'll never forget how Shawn interacted with my niece and nephew, especially my nephew. He did silly voices and impressions and my nephew laughed and laughed. Then, he made Shawn repeat the performance. I couldn't believe this nineteen-year-old guy could be so good with kids. He was so patient, so kind.

The first time we went to his dad's for dinner I felt so nervous. Shawn kept telling me not to worry; he had told his father all about me and everything would be fine. He was right. Shawn's dad really rolled out the red carpet for us. We had cocktails before dinner, followed by the most amazing meal. His dad was funny and engaging. I swear the conversation didn't lag once. It seemed as if he had been planning this night for ages with only the two of us in mind. He made me feel like a special member of the family. My anxiety at visiting Shawn's father disappeared. Instead, I looked forward to it with gusto. This period was good.

We didn't have much time together because we worked opposite shifts. We were like ships passing in the night. For a while this scenario worked, but absence didn't make my heart grow fonder; it made me feel lonely. I was nineteen and I wanted someone to spend my free time with, someone to share my life and my thoughts with. Shawn was never around and when he was, he partied with his friends. After much soul-searching, I decided to end my relationship with Shawn. I didn't think it fair to stay when my heart wasn't there anymore.

My sister and mother both thought that Shawn and I would eventually marry and settle down, even after we broke up. Whenever that came up, I laughed.

"There's no way I'm going to marry Shawn," I said. "He's just not the right guy for me."

I wanted someone older and wiser. I wanted adventure–a challenge! My sister merely nodded and smiled. If I thought that was the end of it, I only kidded myself.

Shawn left the Madison shortly after our break up, and time marched on. About a year later, I heard that Shawn's dad had passed away. All I could think about was this lovely man who had opened his home to me because his son had wanted him to. I knew Shawn would be devastated. I tried to reach him but his number was no longer in service. At the funeral, he looked so lost, so broken. I tried to talk to him afterwards but he appeared to be in another world. I did get his new phone number so I could call him, but he was never home and he didn't return any of my calls. Later I learned that he had gone traveling to clear his mind and escape from reality for a while.

Years passed. I dated on and off, even becoming serious with one or two men, but these relationships always came to an end. During this time, Shawn and I occasionally ran into each other. This was the norm when you work in the hospitality industry and hang out with bar people. The type of hours and days of employment make it difficult to maintain friendships with people outside of the industry. For some former couples, these run-ins may have proved awkward, but never for us. We were always happy to see each other and we'd spend the rest of the evening catching up. Because we were friends first, I found it easy to slip back into that role. I can remember ending up at his place a few times after such meetings, and we would talk into the wee hours of the morning, but it never went any further than that.

More time passed. We would call each other sometimes to see what the other one was up to. One particular phone call came as soon as I walked in the door. It was Shawn.

"How are you? he asked.

"Fine," I said. "How are you?"

"I'm in the hospital," he replied.

I completely freaked out. I could feel my heart in my throat. I guess he could see where this was going.

"I'm fine," he said. "I've suffered a blood clot from a broken ankle but I'm fine now. Don't worry. I was thinking about you while recovering and I just wanted to hear your voice. I heard you're dating someone and just wanted to know if you're happy."

"I am."

However, I wasn't, but it didn't seem right to complain about it at the time. We chatted a little while longer, and then he said he had to go.

It wasn't long after that when my mom mentioned that he was working at The Madison again (I had left a few years earlier to work at my sister's new bar). I have to admit my heart skipped a little at this information. Some time had passed since I had spoken to him and I wasn't all that sure I even knew what I wanted out of our "relationship" anymore. I ended up talking myself out of going to see him because I wasn't certain about the way I felt.

On Sunday June 15, 1997, at about 4:30 p.m., my whole world changed forever. As I headed out the front door on my way to work, the phone rang. I was running a little late but answered it anyway. Immediately I knew something was wrong. It was my niece on the phone and she sounded frantic. She told me that her mom (my sister) had collapsed at home and was on her way to the hospital. I don't actually remember the cab ride to the hospital; I just remember arriving there and seeing my brother-in-law's face.

My sister had suffered an aneurysm and was bleeding into her brain. There was nothing the doctors could do. They kept her as comfortable as possible. She passed away on June 18, 1997. I was devastated. I still miss her more than words can say. We had a wake for her the following Friday and Saturday. I don't recall much about the wake or that whole month. Much of that time is a blur.

One occurrence at the wake I will never forget. As I walked aimlessly around the room, feeling lost, I noticed Shawn at the front door, about a hundred feet from where I stood. The whole room...the room that was full of at least fifty people, maybe even as many as one hundred...seemed to fade into the background. The room grew quiet the very instant his eyes found mine. For that moment it was as if there was no one in that room but us. All I could see was his kind and loving face so full of concern and relief at my relative well-being that my heart completely melted. The distance between us evaporated as he rushed to me and gathered me into his arms. If anyone understood the relationship between my sister and me, Shawn did. He could instantly comfort me in a way that no one else could. There was something about Shawn that night, something about the way he looked at me from across the room that made me realize he loved me with all of his heart. Always had, and always would. I also realized that I loved him too and in a way I hadn't before or couldn't have before. I wasn't that naïve girl any longer. I knew my own heart and that heart belonged to Shawn.

Sometime later, Shawn said he had something to talk to me about and asked if I remembered the day he had called me from the hospital. He said that the blood clot had nearly killed him that day. The doctor had informed him if he hadn't come to the hospital as soon as he did, he likely would have died in his sleep. He kept this information from me because he thought I was in a happy relationship, and that telling me wouldn't have been right under those circumstances. When he realized how close he had come to dying; the first person he thought of was me and he regretted never having told me how much he loved me, how he had known, for some time, that I was the only one for him. He had just been waiting for me to figure it out.

"If you ever considered marriage, would you consider marrying me?" he asked. "There is nobody in the world I love or care about more. I will love you always."

By this time, I was crying and telling him that I loved him too. We were hugging and kissing and crying all over the place.

I feel very strongly that my sister was instrumental in my seeing the truth of that love on Shawn's face that day; which in turn, opened my heart to a truth of its own. She was right about Shawn. So was my mother. They saw what I couldn't see – this wonderful man who happened to think the world of me. How completely blind I had been.

We were married on October 15, 1998.

# Resonance

I first met Howard in 1978 in Arizona at Rainbow Gathering, a community of 10,000 people. We were on a piece of land out in the middle of nowhere, with the sole way in being a long hike. You had to bring not only what you needed to survive on the land for your stay, but you had to give something back to the community. I had traveled there with some friends from Cloud House Poetry Center in San Francisco.

Howard was one of only two people that I met there who exhibited a special, very attractive energy to me. We both worked in a food group. One day as we hiked from the kitchen area to the eating area, a friend led us in a song. I carried a bunch of pitted cherries on my shoulder and Howard trekked ahead in the line. While we walked up the hill, his voice flowed back over me. His voice was deep and it had a timbre that resonated with me. I thought *Oh, what a beautiful sound and what a beautiful voice!* From that moment I was drawn to him.

The next time I saw him, a few days later, was right after I had attended a rebirthing seminar. At the workshop, many of us had been partnered for simultaneous rebirthing. During the session I had felt my nerves seize up and then break through the block into clear mode. From that state of mind, that state of heart, I returned to my camping spot. Poets were reciting their poetry around a campfire someone had started. Then Howard showed up carrying a guitar and began to sing. I could see what he sang was more than words – it was the tone of his voice and his delivery. His song came from deep inside and had so much beauty that I wanted to be part of it in some way. I knew some sign language so I started signing his words back to him across the fire. He looked up and he noticed me signing. He saw me exactly as I was, completely rebirthed, completely open, and hearing who he was and what he had to say. As he sang, I sensed his inner being. I felt that he longed to be one with me, that he craved love. I could feel through the way he sang, through the opening of his voice, that chest-rumbling sound that is his voice.

After the campfire sharing, I got sick and didn't see him again for the remainder of the gathering. I thought, *Well, that's it then.* I returned home to Santa Cruz.

About two months later I heard that a group of people from the gathering were coming to do a festival in San Lorenzo Park in downtown Santa Cruz. So I went and there he was. When I saw him I started signing to him because somehow I thought he knew sign language. He had mimicked me back at the first camp. He knew who I was and I knew who he was. I felt overjoyed to see him again. However, I was still somewhat shy.

We took part in an ortho-bionomy workshop which included massage. I felt his touch. I felt the depth of love in him. I was still a little too shy so I let the opportunity to get to know him better pass.

During the next few days I met him again on a beach. He ran around trying to get a huge banner to stand up against a teepee. The wind from the ocean kept scooping and blowing this way and that. The banner showed two hands holding the earth and read *Protect, Respect, Celebrate.*

Howard had the spirit to set himself an unbelievable task that a reasonable person would never undertake. I loved that persistence about him. Again I felt who he was inside. Again I didn't invite him anywhere because I still felt shy and hesitated putting myself out there. However, I was really interested.

A day or two later I ran into him a third time when he was shopping. I realized that he didn't have a lot of money and that his life wasn't running smoothly. I thought, *What this guy needs is a good home-cooked meal.* So I invited him home.

He had a swollen knee and walked with great difficulty. I did some massage and I worked on his knee. I fed him and showered him and fell in love with him. I invited him to stay and he did. He moved in with me. It took us eight years to commit to marriage, but we already had the relationship. We've been together for thirty-two years.

I am the happiest when I'm with him. There's an incredible feeling of comfort when I put my head on his chest and he hums in his deep base voice. To me, his vibratory resonance of voice goes beyond words. This resonance exists in both of us in many ways – the touch aspect, the sound of our voices and the joy of singing together, the ability to talk about anything at all to each other, the love that is bigger than frustration. He is someone I can count on. With Howard, I get the feeling that I can surmount difficulties even when I don't know how. I suddenly find that a way always exists when there is love.

# Part Two

# Family! Gotta Love 'em!

## Love and Laughter

I come from a long line of short men with bad hearts.

Well, that's my opening line at least. I am the youngest of ten children, nine boys, one girl. She was the second oldest. Everyone after Richard Alan Jr. was supposed to be Monica, but it never quite seemed to work out. My sister is a psychologist now, which makes sense, I guess. I tell people my parents stopped when they got it right.

I'm about 5'6" and that height is average for my brothers, hence the long line of short men.

My father had a heart attack when I was two or three years old. Apparently he had to stay home while my mother tried to keep the kids quiet. She was good, but no one is that good. He had a couple of other heart attacks in his life, and several procedures to keep the blood flowing. My mom had a pacemaker put in when I was in seventh grade. So, from Dad we inherited plumbing problems and from Mom, electrical issues. I think I am one of only two right now who do not have a pacemaker, or a pacemaker / defibrillator / wireless data recorder / microwave oven implanted it their body.

Hence the bad hearts.

I figure the above is a more original description of a family than a large mid-western Catholic repressed testosterone factory. That all seems somewhat cliché. Oh, and Irish. Can't forget the liquor.

"Oh my God, what's it like to grow up in a family that big!" is usually the first question. No, the second. The first is, "Are you Catholic?" Unless you are on the west coast, then the first questions is, "Are you Catholic or Mormon?" But back to the 'What's it like' question. I have no idea. It's the only way I grew up. I don't have another childhood to compare mine to.

Although my mom tried–comparing, that is. I remember most of my childhood as a time when Mom would compare us to the "nice" families. The "nice" families were usually a little WASPier than we were, or Catholic, but with a better sense of rhythm and a smaller more controllable brood.

The "nice" families presented very 1960s houses with front yards that did not have football goal lines drawn in the grass. Cars that were not dented and did not regularly seat more than eight. Nice church clothes that had been previously worn by only one or two of the children. A family picture in the living room. Yeah. It was easy to hate the "nice" families.

But we were no different from anyone else in that we knew all our own dirt, but not all the dirt on the neighbors. It was a small neighborhood, but not that small. We knew how often the police were called to our house to quiet a party when Mom and Dad were out of town. The same thing happened in "nice" families, but that didn't get advertised. In my family the police being called was generally the first thing one of the brothers would say, either to try to get someone in trouble or to try and impress the audience. We were skilled in finding attention amid the crowd.

But what really interests me is how great my siblings turned out. They may have been loud unruly kids, but they became really great adults, amazing parents, and smart business people.

Well, when we would say "I come from a family of ten children" to a mother of a "nice" family, the response was often "Oh, there must have been so much love in that house!"

A typical response from my family was "Love, hell. It was pure competition. I was twelve years old before I knew a cookie could be eaten cold." (Credit: Brother Mark.)

Of course, our family had love; otherwise there would have been homicide. But those words stated above–nine boys (plus Dad), Irish mom, Midwestern, Catholic. These are words that epitomize repressed emotions. The showing of love in this house usually involved the lack of a smack upside the head. Not by my parents; they were never spankers, or hitters. Trust me, with nine boys, you learn to make them cower with your voice, or else you could break a hand. My brothers, on the other hand, were physical. They were boys. So if you wanted something from another brother, it wasn't about sharing or negotiations, it was about threats and intimidation.

I do remember an older brother's "whoever finds my keys gets a reward" trick. We, the little ones would scramble around the house and find the errant car keys, and run to the cool teenage brother.

"Here they are!" we would say. "Here they are! What do I get?"

"Your prize is you don't get hit" was the favorite reply.

One learns quickly not to complain about this prize, because it can be taken back.

Okay, so this is not a touchy-feely family. But it is true that a lot of love existed (still does). It seems the greatest expression of our love was humor. Yes, this is a really funny group of people. And really competitive, so you had to be REALLY funny to get the attention of this crowd.

When in a group who did not know my family, such as when I was away at college, I discovered that people found my comments and stories funny. And I am the least funny one in the family. It was just an odd experience to miss getting out punch-lined every time I said something. Oh, I found funny friends, but never in the close quarter's situation like my formative years.

True it could be a little mean-spirited sometimes. I did have someone in college tell me that he thought I was a little mean with my comments towards people, and that it seemed so negative.

"Pat, I'm sorry you think it is mean," I said to him. "For me the humor is a way of bonding and showing my love. If I make a smart-ass comment to someone, that's just my way of saying 'I love you; I want to be your friend.' It sounds a little mean, but it's just my approach to someone I respect. And, Pat, you look nice today."

It took him a couple of seconds to get that joke.

But the love and humor in my family started at the top. My mom was a riot. I would have loved to hear her in her youth. I'll bet she had the whole crowd in stitches. By the time I came around, we were getting a little older, and she was getting kind of tired (Hey, I said ten kids so of course she was tired), and the humor often came out as a jab to the neighbor, or the actions of one of the kids, or some stupid so-and-so on television.

I do remember a reprimand to the youngest three of us, for some action that could have been dangerous or expensive. Using a phrase that had been common at some point in her life, but was new to us, Mom sternly chastised us.

"That's about as funny as a rubber crutch," she said.

We knew we were being yelled at, but as that visual sunk in, Steve, the second youngest, let out a little snort of suppressed laughter. Then came the shoulder shake of the silent laugh–you know the one. At this point, Dan and I started to visualize the rubber crutch too. The three of us began giggling, and snorting, and then out-and-out belly laughing. She had to join in at that point. I mean, picture the look on the faces of three young boys as they visualize someone trying to use a rubber crutch. It's hysterical.

Steve was probably one of the funniest in the family. He's just three years older than I, and was two years ahead of me in school (I reminded him of that when it was argumentatively useful). This guy knew how to hold an audience. And this family was a tough audience, but Steve was the virtuoso. I mean, he could get away with an imitation of the parish priest because he was so funny, and so spot on, that my parents laughed. It's hard to scold too hard when you have tears of laughter rolling down your cheeks.

As Steve was next in age to me, we had our occasional knock-down/drag-out fights during the school years. When people are close and have arguments, there needs to be the acknowledgement of the "it's all right" after the fire simmers down. Sure there was plenty of ignore-it-and-pretend-it-didn't-happen in my family, but passive-aggressive was not our style. We were more aggressive-aggressive. It was a joke or shared laughter that was the unspoken "Yes, you pissed me off, but you are my brother and I still love you. Jerk," in our house.

Humor not only took our mind off something or broke the tension in the air; humor was also the shared experience, the common language, the intimacy of my knowing the very events and feelings that you know. You see it in the gallows humor of those who have survived some tragic disaster and can laugh at things that others would find unbearable. Like my mother going through menopause.

So, I love my family and I love humor. And all of this takes place in the framework of life, the ups, the downs, etc. We all seemed to get older. Generally fatter and balder too. Well, Steve and K.C. had great hair, and of course, my sister. The rest of us, not so much. And a few kept in shape. I hate those brothers.

My dad died about six years ago, after a long battle with Parkinson's disease. It was really interesting to watch the mature responsible people that my family turned into to deal with this part of life. We now had enough experience with other people, mostly wives, to be able to express love and appreciation. I think we had our time with

Dad before he passed. And that time involved humor as well.

I was standing in his ICU room after another coronary event (I don't know what it was that time, but it clearly was big, if he was in the ICU). Doctors will ask certain questions, especially of patients that could be suffering from dementia, to establish if the patient is alert and, well, here. They will ask "Do you know what year it is? Do you know where you are? Do you know who the president is?" This hospital stay was during the impeachment of Bill Clinton. Dad got the year right, the city and hospital right, and when asked who was president, he responded, "Well I'm not sure. I know who it was when I came in here, but anything could have happened since then." Great. We were here for the ICU examination and got the *Tonight Show* monologue.

After my Dad died my brother Steve was really a lifesaver for my mom. He was not married and lived near her. He made sure she got out and socialized, and of course, he always kept her laughing. It was interesting, because as Mom was the dominant personality in the family, she butted heads with the strongest personalities of her kids, and Mr. Smart Mouth Fast Reply Steve had been one of those who would ignite the wrath of Mom in many years of his young adulthood. But as she was getting frailer his strong personality was just what she needed to tell her when to stop bitching and go out for dinner. Or let's call Cindy, or let's do whatever. Here the love was shown with action, with patience, with compassion, and with humor. His constant comments and jibes kept her going through the stuff that life dishes out.

And here is where the part of my opening line "...with bad hearts" comes back to bite me. At forty-six, Steve suffered a massive heart attack while actually at his doctor's office for a check-up. By this time, many family members had been through heart procedures, or had pacemakers, etc. Much of this heart disease was serious, but all had been treated successfully. Even my dad did not die from heart disease. Steve did.

I was living in California when this drama took place in Minnesota, but most of the rest of the family were there. On the 31st of January, they came together to try to grasp the unthinkable. I was constantly on the phone from California after he went into the hospital, unsure of the status, of his chances, of the hope for a miracle. On February 1st, my family had to take my mother in to say goodbye to her son before turning off the life support.

When my dad died after a long illness the phrase that made the most sense was "It was anticipated but never expected." When Steve died, there were no words.

I flew home and did what I do. I tried to help people. I tried to help my mom. I tried to help with planning and activity. I was with my family.

I went to the same funeral home, the same room that had held my dad's body a couple of years earlier. On my previous visit I had discovered the comfort of a viewing before a funeral. Something not easy to dismiss as morbid when not in my sphere of experience, showed itself as a valuable part of the grieving process when I needed it.

With Steve, I was unsure if I could handle an open casket. I stood in the back of the room simply terrified to go see for real that my big brother was dead. When the opportunity presented itself, I grabbed the arms of one of my older brothers and his wife when they started up to view Steve's body. After a second of not quite getting it, they realized this was my first time seeing him. What I needed was there. Love. Support. Understanding. The safety to feel what I needed to feel. Steve's body did not

146

look better for the wear. While the funeral director did a fine job making the body look good, the heroic measures taken in an attempt to save him had left him bloated and not really like his previous appearance.

Next, I remember when my mother entered the room. My sister was on her arm and they were starting toward the casket. I stepped up and took my mother's other arm to be there, to help support this woman as she viewed the body of her son.

We stepped up to the open casket. In a nice dark suit lay Steve's body, looking familiar but not real. My mother spoke. Her voice was a bit weak, but loving.

"Oh, would you look at him," she said. "He looks so handsome."

"I don't know," my sister replied. "I don't think it looks at all like him."

Without a moment's hesitation, my mom said, "That's because he's not talking."

The three of us began to laugh.

Sean and his wife came up to join us. We shared the smart-ass humor that we all knew Steve would have loved. Sean commented that he had asked if they could transplant Steve's hair to his head.

"Well, he's not going to use it anymore!" Sean said.

I smiled. I cried. I love these people.

It's easy to look back on a family and pick out what bad situation or habit created this problem in my life or that situation I have to deal with. But it's truly joyful to look back on a family and realize the amazing gift of laughter and a wonderful sense of humor that I have received from these people.

My name is Tony. I come from a long line of short people with really, really good hearts.

# A Great Teacher

I was born in 1930 and grew up in the Depression. During that time, my dad was Superintendent of Schools for Bollinger County in South East Missouri. I remember that men would knock on our back door at night, come in and talk to my father. He would give them a few dollars because most of them had no money at all. Although Dad had a large family of seven children, and very little material goods, he did have a school teacher's salary. He took care of so many people and I'm sure that he never received most of that money back. He wasn't the sort of person who really expected it. He knew that these people were extremely poor.

If Dad had an extravagance or an addiction it was probably books. Despite our own meagre economic situation, we always had books. He read to us about things that he found meaningful

I remember sitting on his lap quite often as a young girl as he read in his fine speaking voice. Once he read *The*

*Cremation of Sam McKee* to the whole family. How carried away we all were listening to him. He was so excited about the book and he made the rest of us just as excited. People liked to hear him talk. He expressed himself unusually well.

Even though we were very poor in possessions, we were very rich in what we could talk about, what we could imagine, and what we could dream. He was good at inspiring us that way. He was a great teacher. We talked about many, many different subjects at the dinner table. In that way, we were rich.

At Christmas time Dad went out in the woods near our home and cut down a small cedar tree. We might get one toy of some kind, but of course, we always received books.

Dad never did his Christmas shopping early. He always waited until Christmas Eve. When I was five, my Christmas list contained one item–a Shirley Temple doll. When Christmas morning arrived, a doll sat under the tree, but the doll was tiny and black. Of course, I was so disappointed. My father had assured my mother that I wouldn't care that the doll was small and black.

"No, she isn't prejudiced," my mother said. "It's just that it isn't what she had in mind."

Dad knew I wasn't prejudiced because I had not been taught that at home. When he realized my disappointment, he arranged with the store to order me a Shirley Temple doll for my birthday. My birthday was July 5th.

In the fall, right before school began, I was getting ready to go to first grade. I had one old pair of shoes called Mary Janes. I wore them when my dad and I went to the store to buy a new replacement. It was a general store where they sold everything from baloney to straw hats. Dad told the owner of the store that he had come to get me a new pair of shoes. The owner brought out the new shoes and we looked at them. A man came in with a little girl. She had no shoes at all. She was barefoot. She needed shoes for school too. My father heard what the man said to the store owner. He was trying to buy shoes on credit. However, the man and his family were new in our area and the owner didn't know him and so, wouldn't give him credit. My father volunteered the money that he had planned to spend on my shoes for the little girl to have shoes so that she could go to school.

This was not unusual for my dad. This was the way he reacted to situations. He wanted money to be used where it was most needed. I was disappointed.

"Carmine, you must really feel good about giving that little girl your shoes," he said as we walked home.

When I thought about it, I did. He was a great teacher in many ways.

When I was twelve, my parents got divorced. The year before their divorce, my dad sent my mom to beauty school so that she could make a living. From then on I spent the school years with my dad and the summers with my mother. When my mother died, Dad came to the funeral and explained to me that he had always loved my mother, but he just couldn't live with her. They were so dissimilar and had gone in different directions since they had married.

When I was thirteen, I went to school in Naylor, Missouri where my father was then school Superintendent. One of my friends in my freshman class was fifteen and she became pregnant that year. I remember the day that the information spread all over the school and how dismayed I felt. But my father came to me and put the situation in perspective.

"Carmine," he said. "This is such an unfortunate thing for the girl, for the boy and for the families, but, Carmine, this is not the greatest sin in the world. The greatest sin in the world is greed."

I've never forgotten what he said. Today, here I am at eighty years old, and I look around at the world and greed still is the greatest sin. Greed causes more wars, more unhappiness and distress than anything else. Dad was able to tell me that when I was still a child, which meant, I guess, that he thought we had a pretty good relationship where he felt he could say that to me about my friend and her "sin" as people in the area called it.

In 1986 I went to Dad's funeral in Ada, Missouri. Such an outpouring of people attended. Some of them learned that I was his daughter and they came to me. A woman who had become a nurse said that he had helped her through the first semester when she went away to college. He had paid her tuition. Another woman came up to me and said, "Your father bought my clothes the first year I went to college." People admired his compassion and the way he helped those trying to get an education. He believed that education was the means up and out, and to get ahead.

He was gifted in so many ways, in his ability to explain, to visualize and imagine. He was unusually patient, compassionate and understanding

The first thing I think of as a gift from my dad is the love of learning, that through life you continue to learn, to be adventurous and to get out there and learn new things. I know I've learned compassion. However, I wish I had more of his patience.

# A Tidal Wave of Love

In February of 2001, I came home from University for one week. I found that time in my life especially difficult. I was worn out from too much studying and not enough living. Over the years, I had put too much pressure on myself: to do well in school; to live up to what I thought my family wanted; to be the kind of man I thought my friends wanted and to stick to the impossible standards that I set for myself. It wasn't until years later that I realized how toxic it had all been and how much I had sucked all love from my life. Love was replaced by obligations, responsibilities and other people's perceptions of me. I didn't think I deserved love until I reached some goal that I could never reach.

My sister-in-law was pregnant at the time. I wasn't expecting to be around for her delivery as it wasn't scheduled for another three weeks. So, I was surprised when on my first day back from school, my sister-in-law went into labor. I was worried that the baby would be at risk by being born so early. I was assured that giving birth three weeks ahead of schedule is still safe for the baby.

We went down to the hospital and eagerly anticipated any news. Later that night, my sister-in-law gave birth to a beautiful, healthy baby girl, Priya.

Words can't properly describe how I felt seeing that little miracle for the first time. In the beginning of her life on planet Earth, this tiny little creature with big, beautiful brown eyes looked around the room at all the new faces. I couldn't help but watch her discover the world around her. I was overwhelmed by a feeling that had become so foreign to me. I was overwhelmed by love. Love so strong that it blurred out all responsibilities and all perceived expectations. It was love in its purest sense. It was the love in a newborn and the love that I felt for this special person in my life.

A day or two after she was born, Priya, my brother and sister-in-law came home. My parents were staying at my brother's place and so was I. The entire family was all under one roof and I was present for everything: for the drive to the hospital, seeing my niece a few minutes after her birth, and her coming home for the first time. I also remained there for the rest of the week. Priya slept most of the time in her crib and I watched her for hours.

The true miracle, the true awesomeness of the event is that logically, I shouldn't have been around for any of it. Priya should have been born three weeks later, when I was knee-deep in mid-term exams 200 kilometers away. I should have heard about her birth over the phone rather than having a front row seat. Despite how cruel I was to myself, I was blessed with this miracle of timing. I now see it as one of the most wonderful, unexpected gifts that the Universe has given me.

At the end of my week off, I returned to school with a heavy heart at leaving her so soon, but I was also grateful for having met her and spending that week with her.

I didn't know it at the time, but that little girl saved me. After walking through what felt like a desert wasteland for years, being with her was like a tidal wave. I was hit with so much love at once that I didn't know what had happened to me. Just by being present, Priya taught me what was really important in life. She taught me that next to love, everything else was trivial.

Since then, I've been blessed with four more nieces and nephews–four more ambassadors of unconditional love. Because of them all, unconditional love isn't just some intellectual concept that reads well on paper but doesn't exist in reality. Because of my nieces and nephews I can just think back to any moment that I've had with them and get immersed in that tidal wave again.

# Adopting Nicole

Parenting is not for everyone. To complicate matters, our feelings about whether or not to raise children can change as the years go by. My wife and I had mutually agreed before marrying that we would not have children, for several reasons that seemed valid at the time. Fifteen years later, this decision caught up with me. I was in my mid-forties and felt a persistent sadness about what might have been; it was an ache that wouldn't let go.

As a teacher, I had certainly encountered more than my share of experiences with children. However, teaching is not parenting. As time passed, I began to regret this "let's stay childless" decision, although I was convinced that my wife would be adamant in her refusal to consider parenthood as an option. To be fair, her biological clock had struck midnight, so giving birth was out of the question.

I found it increasingly difficult to remain sanguine about our childless state. To hear the laughter of children at the beach, or see families at play in a park or enjoying a meal together engendered feelings of shallowness and yes, envy. The faces of destitute kids on TV commercials for World Vision left me longing to connect with even just one.

At our stage of life, adoption was the only real choice. As we were now in our early fifties, international adoption remained the sole possibility. The only way we could rationalize bringing a toddler into our lives was to consider the alternative–what would life hold in store for a native Guatemalan baby given up at birth by a parent too poor to care for her?

Financial considerations were not insignificant. In our case, including visits to Guatemala, foster care and legal fees, we looked at adoption costs of between thirty and forty thousand dollars. Combined with a mountain of paperwork, not to mention approval from a government-certified social worker, we discovered that international adoption is not for the faint-hearted.

What trumped all the difficulties was a one-by-three inch photograph of our potential "daughter-to-be," sent by our adoption lawyer. The photo showed a slightly grainy black and white image revealing the face of a beautiful, innocent baby.

It's impossible to describe the emotional impact of this photo. To view a picture of a child whom you've never met, with the understanding that this child might become part of your life and family, overwhelmed me, in a most beautiful, powerful way. Who can explain it? All I know is that I began to love our future daughter while looking at that photo. I carried it in my wallet for months.

We were given the choice to accept or decline adoption proceedings. I didn't hesitate. Nicole's was the first and only photo we needed to see.

Once we had committed to adoption, our world started to change in a myriad of ways. Purchasing or receiving baby items such as a crib and high chair, and creating an additional bedroom in our townhouse by subdividing and decorating a larger space were tangible, exciting, but slightly scary reminders about the future that awaited us.

To complicate matters, we experienced significant paperwork delays. What we had hoped might happen in six months stretched to almost a year of waiting and wondering. One of our documents had sat in a consular office for weeks, because it was short a few postage stamps on the return envelope. The consular had not bothered to let us know.

To help finance our adoption, I took on two part-time jobs, as well as continuing my fulltime teaching position. This became very stressful, particularly when my father, in his eighties, deteriorated quickly physically and died during a brief hospital stay. At the same time, my mother developed non-Hodgkin's lymphoma. It was the most difficult, agonizing period I had ever experienced. I literally had to put myself on automatic pilot to survive emotionally.

The photo in my wallet kept me going, despite doubts about the wisdom of proceeding with adoption.

Nicole arrived at Toronto International Airport on the evening of February 28, 2001. We bundled up our tiny, tired new arrival and headed back home through the chilly night air. At fourteen months, she must have known in a primitive way that something earth shattering had just occurred. I desperately wished I could have explained the situation to her to soften the impact, but at least she seemed to adjust to her new environment with relative ease.

Holding and comforting our own adopted child in my arms was the most profound, meaningful act I have ever experienced. The protective parental gene seemed to "kick in" automatically. My wife and I were no longer two individuals cruising the world in a figurative sense. We had responsibility for the life of our daughter.

Almost ten years have passed since Nicole arrived in Canada. We have weathered our share of ups and downs...with many more ups by far. From the "get-go," a wonderful older couple from our church in Toronto unofficially adopted Nicole as their love grandchild and continued treating her as their own. She has been blessed with good health and an active mind. Later this year we will travel to Australia so that Nicole can bond with my wife's side of the family.

To be sure, adoption is a big deal for a child. Nicole also has to deal with being a visible minority member in a predominantly white community. All things considered, however, we think that she is generally thriving and will develop into a fully engaged, and hopefully, happy, member of the community.

In the meantime, she sometimes asks, "Why do you love me Daddy?

"Because you're you," I reply.

My answer seems to satisfy Nicole's need for reassurance. It's the truth–a truth that I am privileged to repeat every night at bedtime when I tuck her in.

"Good night, Nicole...love you."

"Good night Dad. Love you too."

It doesn't get any better than this.

# Adoption: a Love Story

My love story began the moment a thirteen-day-old sleeping baby girl was placed in my arms. After six years of waiting the day had finally arrived, I was a mother. The instant I saw her I knew this was my child, born of my heart. Inside I thanked the young woman, the mother who made this possible. This incredible gift was a cherished child and each night I would tell her about how she came to us, her love story.

Our friends and neighbors were very excited for us, and had waited for our arrival with her. It was early evening when we got home. Since she had been placed in my arms a few hours earlier her eyes had not opened once. Our initial awkward attempts in putting her in the car seat did not disturb her.

As we pulled into the neighborhood and friends came to see our sweet baby girl, she continued to sleep as we tenderly passed her around. This scenario continued into the next few days, with this darling bundle sleeping as she was admired and held. The house became filled with pink and white packages, baby quilts lovingly and especially made for our darling daughter. It was truly a celebration of a new life and love!

Each year on my daughter's birthday I especially thought of the young mother and wished I could share with her the delightful child that tiny baby had become. Sometimes my daughter would stand in front of the mirror and wonder what her birth mother was doing or if she looked like her. I would respond with answers I imagined possible– she had finished university, was working, and maybe married. I knew someday she would meet the woman who gave me the first of two of the greatest gifts in my life.

Jumping ahead a few years, my daughter was busy with university and had talked about a possible reunion with her birth parents at some point. She received a letter saying one of her birth parents would like to make contact with her. We both felt it was her birth mother. At first I thought I would be graded on the most important test I had ever taken. My daughter was both lovingly concerned about my reaction and excited. The initial contact came by email through a social worker. This quickly led to phone calls; then the plan for a first meeting between them.

The week before this meeting, while on vacation, we talked about a gift for her birth mom. As we are a crafty family, I suggested we create a scrapbook of my daughter's life especially for her birth mom. We spent the evenings sharing so many memories as we put the pages together and looked back over her childhood through photos and mementoes. This was my love story, sharing my daughter's life and lovingly offering it in the pages we created of her life, our lives together. I felt even closer to my daughter and to the young woman who gave me this life to love.

The reunion of my daughter with her birth mother was very special. It brought my daughter more family to know including biological grandparents living only an hour away. Our initial meeting with her birth mom, grandparents, half sister and brother was at a picnic. At first we all felt nervous, but we had so much to share with our common bond. My daughter's biological mom had the same beautiful smile, hair, and tan. They looked like sisters. So many questions were answered for my daughter.

How did I feel?

I felt blessed to be part of this reunion and to find my daughter, always a student and seeker, discover what she had looked for and wanted to know. The question I have been asked almost without exception and always with concern was "How do I feel about this?" My response is "When we have more than one child, we do not love the first one less; we love each child as much, and with each, have a unique loving relationship. My daughter, now being in a loving relationship with her birth mom, does not mean I am loved less. Our relationship is its own loving one as it always has been. Our love has been only been deepened. I am her mom."

Having more people who love and cherish them is a gift we all want for our children. Now several years later she has also reunited with her birth father and more family. She has had many visits to both families and they also have reconnected. My daughter's story is a loving one and not everyone's story, but as adoptive moms our role is to be loving and supportive throughout this journey. We will always be their mom, but as we taught them to share so long ago, so must we. In doing so, love returns tenfold.

Debra Quartermain
www.debraquartermain.com

# Elaine

"I don't have any friends," my seven-year-old sister Elaine said, sobbing.

I stood there, a six-year old girl, two years younger than my sister Elaine. I was watching as our mother sat with her on the stairs, her arm around Elaine's shoulders.

"No one wants to play with me." Tears ran down her cheeks.

My mother held her. Her face looked sad and she had no words to comfort Elaine.

"I have friends," I said. The words felt like betrayal. It wasn't the first time I had wanted to distance myself from her, and it wouldn't be the last time I would reject her.

So much anger and unhappiness seemed to dwell in our home with Elaine the focus of these emotions. Our family consisted of Mom, Dad and their three daughters. Elaine, born in 1944, two years before me, was the oldest. I was the middle girl and my younger sister, Donna, was the baby, born four years after me. We each had our roles in the family: our little sister the sweet and lovely one; me the selfish one, and Elaine the angry, troubled girl.

One day when I was five, Dad took Elaine and me over to our grandmother's house. Our six wild boy cousins were also there. I thought these boys were great to play with and I really wanted them to accept me. We were all playing outside together when one of them started to yell at Elaine,

"I hate you!" he said.

The others quickly joined in on the attack.

"I hate you!" I also said. Dad charged out of my grandmother's house, telling me it wasn't right to say that about my sister. I looked up at my father as he stood there, helpless.

When I was six my parents bought us a swing set. One beautiful, sunny day Elaine and I played outside on it when our little sister, who was just a toddler, walked in front of us. We hadn't seen her, so the swing whacked her in the face. Of course, there was blood. Now my father took a turn at yelling.

"Elaine, it's your fault!" he said. "You're the oldest and you should have known better. You should have been watching her!"

Terrified, I watched Dad spank Elaine. I felt a terrible sense of guilt and injustice. *I did it too. Why is she the only one getting punished?* I stood there, frozen, wanting to protect her, but unable to do anything.

On other occasions, Elaine heard those words from my father as he spanked her or yelled at her. My father treated her harshly but he left me alone. She grew into an angry child who often took out her fury when we played together. She teased me unkindly and maneuvered herself into the leader position for our games. Sometimes she took my toys and said they were hers, although we both knew better. Often I was angry with her and I resented her.

Dad was frequently out with his buddies, golfing, fishing, and at football or hockey games. He was a guy's guy surrounded by a wife and three daughters. Our boy cousins thought he was the greatest. He took them to the games and out on the golf course. Once we reached puberty, he spent little time with us.

When Dad was home, the dinner table turned into a fight ring where he and Elaine held loud verbal matches. As a young teenager she kept a packed suitcase under her bed.

For me, piano practice was acute torture, but Elaine loved to play the piano. She enjoyed writing, especially poetry. In high school, she walked into the head office of the regional newspaper, *The St. Catharines Standard*, and suggested to the editor that she write a weekly column for teenagers. He gave her the job. Every Saturday she went downtown, reluctantly taking me with her on Mom's command. She and I hung out around Diana Sweets Restaurant while she got her interviews for her column. I admired her for her gutsiness in obtaining that job. In my mind I raised her to celebrity status. But I also loved tagging along and getting to hang out with real teenagers.

However, most of the time I didn't admire Elaine, but felt angry at her. We had no peace at home. She and our father always fought. At that time, I knew nothing about making one member of the family the scapegoat.

After high school I studied art at Pratt Institute in New York. Elaine went to Manhattan to study theatre. I lived in Brooklyn and she lived in Manhattan, but despite our geographic closeness, I didn't want to see her. One weekend, she arranged to come to my school to visit me. I spent time with her but resented having to do so. I cringe now when I remember how I treated her then.

After my year at Pratt I returned home to St. Catharines and attended teachers college. The following year, when I turned twenty-one, I moved to Toronto. My parents helped me get an apartment. I was happy to have my independence and the chance to explore my own life. Soon, however, against my wishes, both Elaine and Donna were living with me.

"Family first," Mom said. "Blood is thicker than water."

I didn't fight it, but I wasn't happy.

During this time, Elaine wrote two small books of poetry, which were published. I liked her poems and felt proud of her creativity, talent and intelligence.

However, within that year everything else began to take a turn for the worse. I found living with Elaine in that apartment miserable. She seemed in a constant rage. One weekend she took a trip to Montreal to visit some friends. Four days later she returned to Toronto. A cab pulled up in front of our apartment building with her in it. When she exited the taxi she was babbling incoherently. She managed to get out that she had attended a party where someone slipped something into her drink.

From that point, life went further south. Our desperate parents started with Elaine on the journey that would take them through the rest of their lives, from one doctor to the next, from hospital to hospital, from treatment to treatment.

Elaine was labeled schizophrenic. She was paranoid, heard voices and behaved in a bizarre manner. She was locked in more than one hospital for the mentally ill, given shock therapy, and drugged heavily. We all visited her regularly, and found it so painful to see her this way.

At one point, the doctors released Elaine from the hospital. She lived in a rented room in Toronto. She met a man whom she lived with for a few years, but she wasn't functioning well and became pregnant. My father was seventy, too old to raise a child. The beautiful baby girl was given up for adoption. Elaine became pregnant again, this time delivering a bright-eyed boy. The pain of giving up her grandchildren was almost more than our mother could bear.

Elaine talked to her voices. She was paranoid of people on the street, calling out some accusation to them. She couldn't care for herself properly, often didn't wash, and she smelled. I was embarrassed, ashamed to be seen walking with her. How could I explain to people who stared, startled as she approached them? I spent much of that time filled with these emotions.

She lived with my parents for awhile, but it became too disturbing. My father, who was old, knew that they had to make other arrangements for her. He and Mom needed to know that she would be taken care of when they were gone. Dad managed to have her made a ward of the Crown. She was given a place in a group home near them in St. Catharines. They saw her every week, and Donna and I often went to visit her too.

Our father died, and then our mother. Two years later. Elaine continued to reside in her group home. When Elaine started falling Donna and I decided to bring her to live in Toronto. We arranged accommodation for her in a nursing home in my neighborhood so that I could visit her easily.

By advocating for her, I arranged to get her living on the first floor where she had the privilege of leaving the nursing home to go around the neighborhood. On a few occasions she went AWOL and made it, by bus, to St. Catharines and back on her own. St. Catharines is seventy miles away. She knew if she asked permission to go it would be refused and that was not the answer she wanted. "Why should I have to ask people to go where I want?" was her attitude. Part of me was in dismay because I feared she would be locked up on the third floor. Part of me cheered for her because through all the harshness of her life with this illness, with all the medications that played havoc with her body and slowed her mind, her spirit and her will remained.

Unfortunately, her last trip without permission or notice landed her in a locked ward of the nursing home. I advocated for her and thought that the nursing home director would return her freedom bit by bit. Going AWOL, leaving without signing out or telling a staff member where you were going was serious but shouldn't result in a life sentence.

After Elaine had been in a locked ward for eight months I requested a patient care conference, which is a meeting of all staff involved with her care. I wanted to find out when they would start to return her freedom. The staff at that meeting informed me this would never happen. Any time she left the building she would need to be accompanied by another adult. I was in shock. I felt enraged and totally powerless.

That was the beginning of another part of this journey. It started with many tears and sleepless nights for me. I prayed a lot, asked for help and guidance. One day, when I visited Elaine at the nursing home, a young woman approached me and introduced herself. She was a nurse. She knew Elaine and her situation. She told me my sister should not be on that ward. This wonderful, compassionate woman became my ally and guide through the maze I entered to help Elaine. Without her I wouldn't have known where to start or whom to talk to.

I visited other nursing homes and a group home. I spoke to many people who continued to guide me and encourage me. I found advocates who spend their time in an effort to protect the vulnerable. Bless them; they are angels.

I found one advocacy group with retired lawyers who donated their time and knowledge to help protect seniors. I talked with a lawyer there who told me that the nursing home's treatment of Elaine was illegal and she wrote a letter to them.

I look at the role of the staff of Elaine's nursing home and realize the situation there mirrors my family as it operated when I was growing up. Like the people in my family, the staff is made up of good people. When Elaine broke the rules they stopped seeing her as a gentle woman who deserved care and compassion. They, like the people in my family, chose to see her as "the problem," someone who made their lives more difficult. They did not act in consciousness. They did not stay in their hearts and so, they did harm.

As Elaine has gone through her journey through her illness, I have also gone through my own journey. Sometimes, I have felt the need to distance myself from her illness. *I, after all, am the healthy one* I tell myself. I know that thinking this way does both of us a disservice. Some days I've remembered this; some days I've forgotten. From anger and resentment, a lack of consciousness on my part, embarrassment, shame and sorrow, I have emerged at love. I have been fierce in my determination that my sister has the best life that is possible. By acting as her advocate I have been able to lay aside the guilt I have felt about not being in my heart with her in the past.

I see Elaine every week. She is medicated. She can speak to me in a normal way but often speaks in words that are significant to her and meaningless to others. She is gentle now but still shows some spirit, not always in the best way.

Elaine has taught me about love in a way that no one else has. I have learned, through her, to give love. We are linked on this journey through life, as sisters.

She is always so glad to see me, so happy with whatever I do for her, with her. I feel humble. She is my teacher.

# Geneviève
(Papa's special gift)

About a week after my daughter Geneviève was born I was holding her and began to cry uncontrollably. Right then I realized that my dream of having a beautiful perfect baby girl had come true. The first week, chaos ruled. My wife Barbara and I existed in the whirlwind that comes with a new arrival. But now I was enjoying my first quiet time alone with my new daughter. In that instant, I thought about how I had worried so much about what could have gone wrong from early on in the pregnancy to the delivery. And I realized that up to now I had continued to focus on these negative thoughts. In that quiet moment, the clouds parted and the truth shone through. Everything had gone well and I was holding my precious baby girl. I was overcome by a wave of gratitude and love.

This epiphany was the first of many wonders Geneviève would teach me.

During the time Barbara and I were expecting, I looked forward to all the things that I was going to teach and show Geneviève. What I didn't see coming was how much I would learn from her. And those lessons started early.

When Geneviève was about three months old and lying in her bassinet, she gazed up at her teddy bear mobile and began to smile. I learned then and there that we discover joy on our own. Don't get me wrong. I was thrilled the first time I made her laugh, but I was doubly thrilled to realize that she could find things on her own that made her happy. She is such a ray of light, laughter and love. And laughter always accompanies moments of discovery for her. She laughed the first time she sat up by herself and she had a terrific "EUREKA" laugh yesterday when she did math for the first time. I love that she sings every day. Sometime she simply sings to get from one place to another and sometimes she just sings for the joy of singing. She has this great musical soundtrack always playing. Geneviève is a constant reminder of how great life is.

Of course, times occur when she isn't happy or I am not happy and that is when I have learned, and continue to learn, that my words and actions have immediate consequences. In those moments, I can see her scared or sad reaction to an angry word I've said or gesture I've made. I have discovered how important it is to apologize to her and reassure her that I regret any words or actions said or done in moments of anger or frustration. It is easy to love and be calm when all goes well; however, remaining calm and loving when all is not well is the best way to show her that I love her unconditionally. And when I have to lay down the law as it were, I have learned that the point always comes across better if I don't shout and rant. In these tense moments, she has taught me to breathe and remember how precious we are to one another.

I never expected my love for Geneviève to be so bittersweet. What I mean by that is everyday has an instant when I recognize that she has stopped doing or saying something as she previously did. That is the bitter part. The sweet part is she always replaces the old with something wonderful and new, which serves as a testament to how she is growing and achieving amazing things. We never read pop-up books anymore but she can follow, and is beginning to read chapter books. This year at the Canadian National Exhibition we hardly spent time in the children's section of the Midway with all the cute kiddy rides. However, she was tall enough and brave enough to go on some of the "Big Rides" with me. And she again gave her laugh of discovery!

Every time I look at her, I see her as she is now, but I also see her as she looked as a newborn or a two-year-old or when she was in junior kindergarten. And in this same instant, I am so grateful that I could stay at home with her because I was able to witness and be part of countless moments in her life. Now that she spends the better part of her day at school, I can see how lucky I was to have her teach me the importance of living in the moment. Otherwise, I never would have learned that a walk taking five minutes to get from point A to point B can also last an hour if you stop to visit with each dandelion, ant or dog you encounter on the way. Now I have moments like that one forever.

I had always heard about unconditional love, but until Geneviève came into my life I had never experienced it. Now I know what it means. It is the most important lesson she has taught me. I would do anything to make her happy and safe.

When I hold her in my arms all is right with the world. Living with Geneviève continues to be a great adventure. I always remember that it started when my dream came true and she came into my life, a perfect beautiful baby girl.

# Leading With Loving Kindness

This is our story. We grew up in two different family environments. While both sets of parents loved us, our experiences with love were very different.

**Jonathan**

For me, growing up in a traditional Chinese family with an older brother and two older sisters was full of strict rules and orderly behaviors. Dad worked long hours as a bartender and Mom stayed home and cared for us kids. Religion and spirituality were not discussed nor taught by my parents. A strict and orderly approach to life was not restricted to parenting. Mom and dad's respective parents had brought them up living life this way and that's what they knew. So when my parents started their family they didn't mess around. My mom had four kids in five years! I definitely felt loved as a kid. The love wasn't so much an affectionate or playful type, but more a providing and caring type, and it also felt very conditional. When I listened and followed directions and rules, I was a "how

186

doy"–"good boy" in Cantonese. When I
fooled around too much and didn't listen, I
received my mom's angry stare–it was
enough to stop me dead in my tracks! As a
result of my upbringing, I became a caring
person but this was quickly overshadowed
by my strong ego. I believed that I needed to
control everything and everyone in my life. I
was thoughtful and caring, but it was very
difficult to let down my guard and receive
authentic love.

**Lauren**

I have mixed feelings about my
childhood. My dad was Jewish and my mom
was Catholic. Although they did not practice
any form of religion, I was exposed to
Judaism because I spent a lot of time with
my grandparents. I was and still am a very
free-spirited person. When I was three years
old, my mom became an alcoholic. For me,
living with her resembled a roller coaster
ride. When she drank she was cold and
mean. Most mornings she expressed remorse
to my younger brother and me. I remember
my mom often telling us we were the best
part of her life. When she was sober, if I
accepted her apologies, she was affectionate
and caring. However, if I showed
disappointment she ignored me and became
distant. I tried to express affection and love

to her. My dad did his best to shield me from the chaos and hurt that comes from living in a dysfunctional family. He gave me a lot of attention, was playful and supportive, and always tried to create a fun and easygoing home life. Consequently, rules, structure and routines were not reinforced while I grew up. As a result of my upbringing, I spent a lot of time focused on having fun and bringing joy to those around me. While I have so much love inside me to share, I struggle with feeling alone and need people around me to feel secure.

**Jonathan**

I did what was expected of me. I went to university, got married, bought a house, and had a child. I was a hard worker and knew that if I wanted to succeed in life it was up to me and no one else to make it happen. Although life was comfortable in a material way and I loved being a father, I felt empty inside. After nine years of marriage, I got divorced. Not surprisingly, my son, Jake, was in so many ways just like me – logical, needed routines, and thrived in a structured environment. While I was a single father, Jake spent his preschool years at a wonderful childcare center. He quickly connected with his teacher who was a beautiful free- spirited person, named Lauren.

**Lauren**

I had a short first marriage. When the relationship became challenging and the joy disappeared, everything deteriorated and eventually I got divorced. I moved back in with my mom and dad. I desperately needed to feel secure and receive their love.

**Jonathan and Lauren**

So how did two people who are very different find themselves drawn to one another and eventually get married? We believe there are no accidents!

**Jonathan**

Lauren's enthusiasm and passion for life broke through my protective exterior and connected deeply with me.

**Lauren**

Jonathan's strong character provided security and safety for me. Before long we bonded in a very deep way and later married. We met each other's needs. After many years of having fun, my dream of having a child came true. William was born.

Of course, life instantly became hectic and stressful: breast feeding was difficult and getting a restful sleep didn't happen. There was very little personal time and arguments started over daily responsibilities. Over a short period of time, we became disconnected. While Jonathan's family tried to help and be supportive, we were not open and honest about our problems.

**Jonathan**

Lauren's family was going through their own life stresses. Her mom's alcoholism was getting worse and the person Lauren relied on most, her dad, was not there for her because of his own depression.

Life became unbearably difficult following the death of Lauren's parents. William was two years old at the time. Even though life for us was falling apart, we managed to keep William as a priority. He was a happy and fun-loving boy.

**Lauren**

Progressively, we fell back on old patterns of behavior learned from our childhood. Jonathan became more controlling and critical in order to cope with the overwhelming stress that he felt. I became very angry and often lashed out at Jonathan. Day by day the close bond was taking a tremendous beating. Showing each other loving kindness was rare and our daily interactions caused further separation rather than opportunities for connecting.

I felt desperate and completely overwhelmed. With no one to turn to, I believed I had no other option but to leave Jonathan. Living separate and apart was extremely traumatic at first, for us. While our husband and wife relationship had fallen apart, our parenting relationship continued to be strong. William made an easy adjustment to having two homes. At this time, William was three years old. On the outside, his physical features looked remarkably like Jonathan's. However, on the inside, he was all me–free-spirited, enthusiastic and loving.

It's amazing that when life reaches what seems like its lowest point, miracles happen. Instead of going down the path of unrelenting guilt and reliving past fears, we managed, although in different ways, to become more open and ready to see life differently. We didn't realize it at the time, but William became our greatest teacher.

**Jonathan**

Spending time with William taught me how to be "in the moment," how to be a kid again and how wonderful it feels to be happy.

**Lauren**

William opened my eyes to appreciate how giving love unconditionally is as important as receiving love. While on my own with William, I learned why following routines and having structure benefits not only him, but me too.

**Jonathan and Lauren**

With these newfound realizations, in our own way, we began asking questions about life. We wanted to find happiness. Each day we discovered that we were more and more open to new ideas and beliefs. We were ready and open to receive. We realized that by letting go of our fears we could allow the authentic love inside us to shine through.

While our upbringing and life experiences put us exactly where we were, it was William's incredible energy and spirit that caused us to begin seeing life through different eyes–eyes focused on leading with loving kindness in all that we do. Eyes, as well, that now see that the doors to true happiness swing inwards.

**Lauren**

Our paths in life are no longer diverging, but steadily converging. We have discovered a new and deeply fulfilling relationship together. Above all, Jonathan is in the process of accepting everyone and everything in his life exactly as they are and as they are not. My intention is to be secure knowing that I can love myself first and that I am magnificent. I also believe that I deserve to receive love and am able to give unconditional love to those around me.

**Jonathan and Lauren**

We know the future is promised to no one. How our relationship evolves will flow from our enjoyment and the decisions we make in the present moment. What we are certain of is that above all else, the source of our energy and state of mind must be more important than what we're doing at any given time. In short, we truly believe that giving and receiving loving kindness is always the answer!

# Mother and Daughter Reunion

**Karen**

I was born in New Brunswick. I came from a relatively normal family but I had a sister, eleven months older, who had special needs. Therefore, my family always focused on my sister. I was definitely an accident, but I also felt that my mother never had time for me because she had the bulk of the responsibility of looking after my sister. Mother and I were like oil and water because I resented not getting the affection I wanted from her. However, I didn't feel unloved. I knew I came from a very good and loving family because I could see the care and concern my parents had for my sister. Yet I was a very unhappy angry kid, precocious, acted out and grew up very independent. As I went through adolescence, I was depressed. I used to fantasize about running away from home, and I couldn't wait to get out of there. I just couldn't see how I fit in with the rest of my family. I went through this period of looking for some place where I belonged. I struggled with this throughout my high school years and into university.

Right after I finished university I had an affair and ended up pregnant. It wasn't dating; it wasn't a relationship. It was with somebody who had actually moved away by the time I found out I was pregnant. It took me awhile to decide, but I knew I couldn't do anything but have my daughter, Marie Josée. At that time, I didn't feel fit as a mother. I knew I was unhappy and angry. I thought that I would pass those traits on to her and that I would be a mean mother. When I was a child my father took the brunt of his anger out on me. He hit me, and I worried that I would do the same to my daughter; I didn't want anyone else repeating my childhood. I had to be a different mother than my mother had been to me.

So I decided to give my daughter up for adoption and went to the social services to talk about what needed to happen. I found out that I could choose everything I desired about the adoptive family. I could be as picky as I wished for my baby. It was important that the mother have time for my child. It was important that my daughter have a good spiritual foundation.

Marie Josée's adoptive parents had been on a waiting list for seven years and were told it might be another three years before a baby came up. However, when I made my restrictive list, they were the only people who matched. They were definitely meant to be her adoptive parents.

My friend attended prenatal classes with me and was present at Marie Josée's birth. My parents didn't respond very well. I think my dad pretended it never happened. My mom would have kept my daughter in a heartbeat. She would have been happy to raise her, but I didn't think that solution was in my daughter's best interests.

In the hospital the nurses let me hold Marie Josée. In that moment the most amazing thing happened. I was enveloped in a white light which felt like God to me. It was like the purest feeling of love that I'd ever felt in my life. I knew that my daughter was going to be all right. It was the most beautiful experience. From then on, there was a complete transformation. My perspective about my life changed and I could see my family in a different light– I realized they had done the best they could under the circumstances. It led to a lot of forgiveness for the pain I had endured all those years. By giving Marie Josée away, I received this gift of learning about forgiveness from her; that was the gift that she bestowed on me.

Twenty-one years elapsed. I chose not to have another child because my sister had genetic mental and physical defects that I could pass on. I had been so happy and relieved when Marie Josée had been born healthy. I didn't want to take any more chances with another child. I didn't focus on marriage; instead I concentrated on my career. I had worried all those years about her health and about whether she had a good family. I always wondered if everything was all right.

I had hoped that someday I would meet Marie Josée, and I could put my name in a registry. I had friends who were adopted. They were in their fifties and sixties, and still hadn't met their birth parents. It never dawned on me that my daughter would be looking for me when she was that young.

My dad and I were trying to place my mother in a nursing home in New Brunswick. We went to the social services office and gave our names. The next day my dad received a call from Social Services. I think that because their office is so small, somebody had a piece of paper on their desk with my last name and they put two and two together. They got in touch with me and asked if I was interested in getting to know Marie Josee. She had put in a request.

The social service people asked me if I would be interested in starting a correspondence with Marie Josée so we did. Social services controlled that contact. It had to be done by letters without exchanging contact information till we signed consent forms. Once Marie Josée and I decided to share this information, we communicated by email.

I now lived in Ontario, but planned to go home to New Brunswick at Christmas, and we decided to meet then. Marie Josée lived about three hours away from my dad. I drove to her place. I was nervous. I didn't know what to expect and worried that my daughter might have felt rejected and abandoned.

When I'd given my daughter up for adoption I'd left her a teddy bear and a letter to let her know how much I loved her and expressing my gratitude that she was joining a loving family. Now, when I arrived at their house, her teddy bear, still in mint condition, sat on a chair near the front door to welcome me. It was clear that they had treated my daughter as if she were a gift.

Her adoptive parents are the most amazing people; I couldn't have asked for better. They have been so welcoming towards me and so inclusive. Because of them, Marie Josée has had a positive attitude towards me her whole life and looked forward to meeting me. She had done poems and art for me when she was younger, and when I arrived she gave them to me. Marie Josée and I were developing a relationship from zero, but they had done so much of the work already to smooth our way. Talk about love. That was a gift they gave to both of us.

When I saw my daughter standing there, for the first time since I'd given her up for adoption, I felt overwhelmed. *She's real, not just in my head,* I thought. All those years I'd just had to imagine. *She's my daughter. I'm her mother.* All of a sudden I could experience her; it was no longer fantasy. My sister had died suddenly, quite young, at thirty-two. Marie Josée reminded me of my sister, and I missed my sister. Seeing how much my daughter resembled my sister and me made that moment so real. Getting to meet Marie Josée was amazing to me.

Her parents had videotaped her entire life–her first communion, birthdays, graduation and special events, so when the time came for her to meet me I could share it. They wrote me the most beautiful letter. Her parents are a gift of love.

Marie Josée has come to visit me too. We are two strangers developing this relationship. We have a natural bond, but we still need to learn each other's likes and dislikes. I mentioned that I like shiny things

"Oh, that's where I get that from," my daughter said.

Through visits and emails we are getting to know each other. The genetic component is amazing; how we turn out is not all environmental. Now it is wonderful having her in my life. When people used to ask if I had any kids, I didn't know how to answer. It was easier to say "No" than to explain it. Now, I proudly say, "Yes, I have a daughter." She is an amazing addition to my life, one I didn't think I would ever get to enjoy.

The day I became a mother again I also became a grandmother. Marie Josée had a baby son, Jessie, not even a year old.

**Marie Josée**

From the very beginning I knew that I was adopted. My mom told me from the time I was a baby and she rocked me to sleep. My favorite bedtime story was about how my mom was at work when she heard the news, how my parents came to pick me up and how they finally got me after all those years. They always told me how much I was wanted. I always felt loved by my parents.

I was curious about Karen, my birth mom. Because of her letter, I knew that she loved me so I never felt resentment or that she had abandoned me. Although young, I remember understanding that she gave me up because she desired something better for me. I wanted to know what she looked like and what her personality was like.

At nineteen, in university, I became pregnant by my boyfriend. I really wasn't ready for kids. I thought I didn't even want kids. I never babysat. I was never around little kids. I wasn't sure if I wanted to keep my baby. I thought about abortion for a split second, but I realized that if my birth mom had done that I wouldn't even be here. For me abortion wasn't an option. It was either adoption or keep the baby. I ended up keeping him because my parents really helped me with my baby and so did my boyfriend and his parents.

Once I became a mother, my curiosity about my birth mother turned into a need. I really wanted her. I knew how strong the bond was that I felt for my baby,

Jessie. I understood how hard it must have been for Karen. I really wanted to meet her. Jessie was six months old when I got the news that I would be able to meet Karen.

When my birth mom came for that first visit I was really, really nervous, but I was excited at the same time. I didn't know what to say. When I saw her I couldn't stop staring.

We've been connected now for over four years. I'm really happy she's in my life, and she wants me to be a part of her life too. We have more of a friendship than a mother and daughter relationship. We are two women who share a common bond and love.

# Standing Strong

Eleven years ago I was divorced and my two sons lived with me. Riley, the younger was three at the time. Once Riley entered school he constantly got into trouble. He wasn't a fighter, but was very bullheaded and acted out in anger when people teased him and that happened frequently. If he made a decision about something he would never change it. From kindergarten through grade eight, Riley got kicked out of school at least once every single year. I don't know how many schools Riley attended in those nine years, but there were several. That situation proved difficult for the whole family.

In grade eight Riley started at a new school again. He had been in school maybe two weeks when he hit a girl because she said something or made fun of him or he thought she did. He just turned around and smacked her. He was hurting.

He got expelled from school. He and I sat down and talked about it. I was truly at my wit's end and didn't know what to do for him. I had prayed and prayed that somehow he would find his way. What ended up happening is that I found mine.

When Riley got kicked out of school I signed him up for some developmental testing to be done. These school-board-run tests could take at least six to nine months to complete. However, Riley had his tests done in under a week. When the test results came back we found out that he had learning disabilities which made it difficult for him in school. He's probably a genius, but some of the ways in which he learns didn't necessarily fit within the traditional classroom.

We were trying to figure out what to do when his principal called. His school had what they called "the bungalow," which was a separate building in the schoolyard. In this building they housed fifteen to seventeen kids with two teachers. It was the only building in that school system which had corporal punishment.

I went to the school and met with the principal because she thought that maybe Riley could go into this program. The other kids in this program were B and E's, had been stealing for years, and had broken the law in many other ways. Some had run away from home; some were into drugs. These were the kids I considered putting my very good boy with. Riley wasn't a criminal; he had anger management problems.

It frightened me to take this drastic action, but I prayed about it. When Riley and I met with the principal and the teachers, it just felt really, really good. Riley and I talked about it. I put him in this program. It was the toughest decision I ever made in my life, but it also turned into the best one.

In this program, my son became the shining star. For the first time in his life he was the kid who tutored all the other kids because of his intelligence. He received all the brownie points while the other kids obtained the demerit points. The other kids turned to him all the time and he excelled. He became this wonderful child.

The school had concise clear boundaries which Riley needed. There was no flexibility – everything was black and white. At home I created the same boundaries, which were *No matter what you do, there's always a consequence.* I made sure that the consequences were natural and reasonable. For instance, he lied to me. A natural consequence to lying isn't grounding. A natural consequence is *I don't trust you anymore.* When I told Riley that I didn't trust him anymore he burst into tears. He was devastated.

"What do I have to do to regain your trust?" he asked.

"It takes time," I said. "You have to tell me the truth even when you're scared to."

We had monthly family meetings. For Riley, the rules were clear, yet reasonable and followed the school's zero tolerance on everything. I never grounded the boys after each turned fourteen, but there was always a consequence when they did something and it always matched the crime.

About two weeks after he had lied to me, Riley asked if he could go to a rave, which I would have said "no" to anyway, but I now had an out.

"You're fourteen years old and I don't trust you," I said. "It would require trust for you to go to this rave."

He got really angry, slammed his bedroom door and cursed at me. It was hard to stay strong, but I did. He came back out of his room about ten minutes later in tears.

"What will it take for you to trust me again?" he asked.

In that moment I almost wept because for the first time, probably ever, I'd reached him.

We worked through the year, and he did really well in school. He finished grade 8. In Alberta you don't go to high school until grade 10. He was going into grade 9 and he desperately wanted to go into another school. I wouldn't allow this to happen. I wanted him to learn that you can build bridges, not just burn them. He'd never had the opportunity in his whole life to know that, learn that, live or experience that condition. So I made him go back into the mainstream school. I found it difficult but I did it out of love. I knew that the best thing I could do for him was to teach him that he is a wonderful person and to see his strength.

He went back into the school. All the teachers and students in grade 9 shunned him because they had been present when he got kicked out in grade 8. So they all looked at him thinking *Oh Riley, big loser.* The first few days he came home in tears

"Honey, you can do this," I said to him. "I know you can. I know how strong you are. It's only one year. Next year you can go to any school you want anywhere in the city. You pick it, but this year you have to build a bridge."

After a month in the school, his teachers started to respect him. Many of them grew to admire him. It would have been so easy to cave in and say, "Okay, honey, you can go somewhere else." By standing strong and believing in his ability to do this, I think I gave him probably the greatest gift of his life. I gave myself a really good one too because I showed him how wonderful he is.

The most fascinating aspect was he completed grade 9 very successfully, with not a single incident – the first year in his history where he had not received a suspension or expulsion. It was probably the first year where he didn't have to change schools or departments in schools. The whole year turned out so great.

In grade 10 he picked a new school where no one would know him. When he started at this new school, magically, his transcripts didn't follow him. Students and teachers thought he was just this funky kid with piercings and a shaved head. They didn't think anything more because they didn't know his history, so they welcomed him. He went in with a clean slate. I believe that is the power of love– when we do what we really believe is right, everything takes care of itself.

My ex-husband, Ken, received a phone call in early December of that year.

When he picked up the phone and found it was the school he expected trouble.

"What did he do?" he asked.

"He didn't do anything," the teacher replied. "It's just that he took this carpentry elective. He's finished his projects already and the semester doesn't finish until February. In grade 10 we don't really like our students to have a spare, so we would like him to choose another elective to fill that time slot."

Ken was just blown away. "You mean he didn't do anything wrong?"

"No, he's great. We really like him."

Ken phoned me in tears.

"Thank you," he said. "Thank you for what you've done for our son."

"We got a call from the school saying you completed your carpentry course with an A," I said when Riley came home from school. "Good job! They now want you to take another class."

"I don't want to. I'd like to have the spare."

"You know what? You've earned it."

I phoned the school.

"He deserves this spare," I said to his teacher.

They didn't know his history and I didn't fill them in. He had earned my trust. He had built his bridges. He'd walked the walk, and I gave him the reward I felt he'd really earned and deserved.

I often think of that time in our lives which was so hard, but the reward was huge. He finished high school and never had an incident. His life turned around and I think it's the power of love. When we love somebody enough to stand beside them no matter what, the answers that we need come through. The direction we need to take shows up, and it all works.

# The Accident

It was a Sunday and we were dressed for church in our matching tweed coats and hats – a pill box for me and a cap for Gord. Those coats were hot and itchy but everyone said we looked cute. I was six; Gord was four, and our youngest brother only a baby on the day of the accident.

When we arrived at the church, Mom took the baby to the nursery. Gord and I waited for her with Dad in the hall close to the church entrance at the front. The men usually hung up their coats in a small vestibule outside the double doors leading to the sanctuary. Dad was placing his hat on a hook as Mom reached the top of the short flight of steps down to the vestibule. It seemed Mom always rushed to catch up to Dad. Gord and I were behind Dad ahead of Mom. She caught the heel of one of her pumps on the metal strip nailed at the edge of the top step. With a short cry, she tripped, spun around, and fell backwards down the stairs. The back of her head hit the wall at the same time as our father turned.

He crouched down beside her.

"Oh my God; Mary, Mary," he said.

Her eyes were closed, her legs splayed in front. Gord and I stood frozen at the top of the steps. Dad shifted Mom towards him and her head fell against his shoulder. Adults gathered in the small space, one talking over top of the other. Someone opened the doors to the church and called, "Is there a doctor? We need a doctor." Others hustled Gord and me away down the hall. We could hear but not see. More shouts, cries, voices. We stood pressed against the wall, numb. Abandoned. The sounds of sirens approached.

"Where are the kids?" Dad asked.

"We'll look after them," one of the parishioners said.

"Find my sister. She'll take them."

Our aunt and uncle drove us to their house for lunch. We did not have to go to church which was good, but Mom and Dad had gone. We would miss going to Murray's Restaurant for pancakes like Dad had promised. Before we ate, our aunt supervised our hand-washing and made sure we used soap. I remember thinking that it was kind of a dumb thing to be worrying about. I didn't want to wash my hands. I was clean when I went to church. Aunt Rita was bossy like Dad. We ate sandwiches on homemade bread, and I tried to play with my cousin in her bedroom. The phone rang and rang. We overheard snippets of the conversations.

"They have to wake her up every fifteen minutes."

"That's to make sure she is still alive," my cousin said.

How did she know?

"The kids?" we heard my aunt say softly on the phone. "They don't know anything."

Later that afternoon, Grandma came to take us home. No sign of our parents, only the orange cat. I checked all the rooms. No explanation of where they were or when they would be home. Grandma made dinner and put us to bed. Our house was a storey and a half with three bedrooms upstairs. My brothers shared a bedroom, and as the only girl I had my own room. It was perfectly placed for eavesdropping, near the upper hall where an open railing allowed sounds and voices to filter up from the living room below.

I made Grandma leave the door to my bedroom open that night. I couldn't sleep and my stomach hurt. Dad came in the front door and I could hear Grandma's voice mixed with his. I crawled out of bed, tiptoed along the carpet in the hall, and peeked through the banister rails. I could see only the two of them – no Mom. They held onto each other in a tight hug. I strained to hear what they said. I didn't want them to see me and get mad at me. Sometimes Dad became angry for no reason. Mom said it was because of the war. He had nightmares about flying his spitfire and yelling at the other pilots in his squadron to dive, dive. My dad liked to be in charge.

Dad and Grandma were a tableau, arms around each other, his shoulders shaking, her blue rinsed hair against his brown. He was crying, a loud choking sound.

"I should have caught her," Dad said. "I should have caught her."

"It wasn't your fault," Grandma said.

I crept back to my bed. I covered my head with the blankets so I couldn't hear more voices or sounds from below. My dad was scared; he loved my mom. He really loved her. I was so scared, but happy. He wanted to save her but he couldn't. He was always able to fix everything. I never heard him cry before; I don't think I ever did again.

Mom came home several days later with a plastic collar to support her neck and head. I liked watching her take it on and off. She had suffered a concussion and whiplash but soon graduated to a soft collar that looked like stuffed socks. My parents went on to have another child, the little sister I always wanted.

Years later when my parents divorced, I wondered about what I had seen that night. What happened to that love? The love that made my dad cry when he imagined losing her. It was there. I know it was.

# The Heart of Love is Truth

One of the hardest lessons I have learned as a man is how important it is to accept Love into my heart, to be an avenue of expression for it so that I may have the greatest possible experience of life. A life with wholeness, meaning, built on authentic relationships with family and friends. Catering to the motivations of the heart is what I believe constitutes a true and pure life. And now that I have learned this lesson, my next challenge is to learn forgiveness. Here is why.

Once I reached my teen years I became what most closely resembles a "troubled youth." I associated myself with the wrong crowd, made very poor choices and essentially drove my parents crazy. My father worked weird hours, so I saw him only on weekends. Until then, it was just my mother and sister to keep me company through the week. My sister and I had a troubled relationship, but it was with my mother that I seemed to have the greatest difficulty co-existing.

My mother was an alcoholic, though thinking back, I could not tell you when her addiction truly began. Unfortunately, I only have memories of the rough times. Memories of when we would fight and argue, of when I would sit up at night wishing she would go away, wishing she would die. I know; what a horrible thing to say. However, at the age of seventeen, I was not mentally capable of dealing with such a troubled human being. As I grew older, her drinking became progressively worse, as did the arguments and fights. We literally were at each other's throats every day and the more I saw her drink the more I hated her for what she put me through. At least, that's how I saw it.

This situation continued for years, and spawned numerous occasions when I had to leave home for an extended period of time just for the sake of my sanity (and probably hers). I had become cold to her. I refused to allow any kind of Love into my heart, any kind of compassion towards this deranged alcoholic. It was commonplace for me to be bombarded with random accusations that made absolutely no sense. From what my father has told me now, much of her problem had to do with her own childhood. On numerous occasions, my

217

father and older siblings intervened and attempted to give her the help and support that we all thought she needed, but we were continually met with anger and denial. She simply refused to change, refused to try.

It was when I reached the age of twenty and was finishing high school that something very real happened. My mother was now "living" off of beer, cigarettes, and Pepsi. She rarely ate, and when she did it would never be something nutritious. She had lost a lot of weight, and for well over two months complained of a sore throat. Because he feared that something might be seriously wrong with mother, my father finally convinced her to see a doctor. After a few days of tests, the results came by telephone and the doctors urged her to return to the hospital. My mother had a cancerous tumor growing in her throat; the tumor by now was somewhat visible. The doctor's prognosis was not optimistic, especially as my mother had not been taking good care of her body for well over a year. She was to start chemo treatment immediately.

At this point, my view of my mother changed slightly. I was still angry with her, but I had become concerned with her condition. Other than the tumor that was slowly becoming larger in her throat, she still had the same negative, angry demeanor I had come to loath. For the sake of remaining civil, I offered my assistance where I could, but did my best to stay away. I still refused to allow Love or compassion into my heart, and therefore still did not SEE my mother for who she was.

A few weeks later, the tumor removed her ability to swallow food or water properly, and she was forced to get an emergency tracheotomy. I still remember the day when I walked into the hospital room, my eyes falling on a withering woman who now had a tube in her throat and no longer had the ability to speak. I don't know if it was how she looked, or the mental realization I would never hear her yell at me again, but I was overcome with a tidal wave of compassion. I could see it in her eyes that she was absolutely terrified of what was happening to her, but she maintained an air of strength.

At one point my mother received permission to return home. Her chemo treatment had slowed the growth of the tumor. With the aid of an oxygen tank and the know-how to suction the mucus from her Trach, we brought her home from the hospital. Our relationship with each other had evolved. Perhaps it was the silence we shared when we sat in the same room, or the small glances we gave each other when others were present. I think it came to a point where we had finally given up on the anger and bitterness, and made some room for sincerity and truth. I was her son; she was my mother. She brought me into this world and gave me life, and I gave her a great sense of purpose and joy. I still don't know when or why we had lost that perspective.

No more than a month passed before she had to be re-admitted into the hospital. Her condition was rapidly deteriorating and it had also become very difficult to care for her at home.-A great sense of frustration was building inside my mother and my siblings. My mother finally asked to be returned to the hospital, where she was placed in palliative care. I visited her as often as I could, coming to the hospital every day after school and staying with her for hours on the weekends. I would sit with her, tell her about my day and what was exciting in my life. Sometimes I read to her, whatever book I was reading; she didn't much care what it was. I think she just enjoyed listening to my voice. Or perhaps she just adored this special time we spent with one another, time that we had missed out on for so many years prior to her getting sick. I had grown to love my mother again, but I also had a great sadness in my heart. I could tell that she did not have much time left. Her eyes conveyed to me that she was "letting go" and accepting her inevitable fate.

One Saturday morning my dad and I had just walked out of the elevator on my mother's floor at the hospital. We made it a few steps before my younger sister came running out yelling, "Hurry up!" She had tears in her eyes. My father and I ran to Mom's bedside, only to find her gasping her last breaths. I broke out in tears, crying hysterically. I screamed out for my mommy, begging her not to leave me. My father was at my side, holding my mother's hand and letting her know he loved her and that it was okay. Her body struggled for a few more breathes. Then she was gone.

This was the hardest moment of my life so far. The woman who for years had literally driven me to insanity and rage, who had tormented me and made my life incredibly difficult was no longer there, nothing more than a lifeless shell. The arrangements were made and my mother was cremated a few days later, her ashes spread at her favorite spot in Algonquin Park.

This experience taught me a VERY valuable lesson. I've learned to not harbor destructive or angry emotions with anyone I truly care for. I learned that once I allowed Love into my heart, compassion into my life, the wicked woman who was my mother ceased to exist. She became a beautiful human being going through a very difficult, personal battle. To this day, I wish I had within me then, the compassion and Love I have for life now. Maybe I would have chosen differently; maybe I would have done more to help my mother. I would have shown her more Love, more warmth. Perhaps she would not have died so young; perhaps my Love would have infiltrated her troubled soul and freed her from the demons which plagued her.

When I kept Love out, all I saw was a false reality. I saw an enemy. I pushed responsibility for my "suffering" outside of me, accepting the role of victim. I failed to perceive my mother as a human being, as a spiritual being. I didn't see her addictions, anger and rage for what they were, a cry for help. A cry for Love. I still have yet to let go of this regret, but in time I'm sure I will learn to forgive myself for being so cold.

I love you Mom.

And that's the truth.

# We've Come This Far

"We've come this far; don't ruin it all now John!"

This cry from my mother was as predictable as what prompted it. All through my girlhood and early teenage years our family traveled a long distance from London, Ontario to the family cottage on Lake Muskoka, a trip undertaken several times a year. Near the end of this tedious journey my father always had his one moment of fun by gunning the car engine and flying over a bump in the highway close to the exit. My brother and I would scream with delight! Our cats, on the other hand, flew off the back ledge of the car and more often than not, threw up. We were in a laughing tangle in the backseat but our frazzled mother was not amused!

This is not to suggest that Mom didn't enjoy a good time. She was truly engaged in living and saw the world through an artist's eye. She loved to paint and could find creatures hidden in branches and stones–everywhere–to the delight of her children, and later, her grandchildren. If you needed someone in your corner she was there. She loved people and spent countless hours listening and talking, often over endless cups of tea. She volunteered and worked hard for many causes from children in a psychiatric hospital to support for abused women. She lived life to its fullest and family and friends loved her zest for living.

I grew up in London, Ontario with my parents and younger brother. Once my brother and I had both married, moved to Toronto and had our own children, my parents decided to join us. What a delight to have them close and especially for my children, to be able to see them so easily. By that time they were in their early eighties and still able to enjoy life and family.

Changes, however, began to creep up on us slowly during their first years in Toronto and were at first difficult to recognize–isolated memory losses that could be attributed to many things. Mom tried to organize a move for them from their Toronto condo to a new apartment. However, she became confused, despite her experience orchestrating many other large-scale events in her life such as charity balls and fund-raisers. Cooking a family dinner was no longer manageable, and we all lamented the absence of the creative birthday cakes that she had baked for all of us over the years. At one point, Mom and I embarked on a project together to build a Victorian dollhouse for her to house her extensive miniature doll collection. It soon became apparent that this project was too difficult because Mom, the artist, couldn't even remember the colors. I was convinced that a serious problem existed and began to understand that the mother I'd known and loved was slipping away from us bit by bit.

We all react differently. My father still denied that there was a problem and my brother struggled to come to terms with it. My husband and children showed great empathy for both Mom and me, and I relied on that to find the courage to move ahead. As so often happens, it takes a serious event to bring a situation to a head. One freezing February night, unknown to my father, my mother left their apartment in a blizzard, dressed in her housecoat, a silk blouse, one slipper and one high-heeled shoe. Fortunately she was reported to the police and taken to the emergency department of the local hospital. However, it wasn't until the next morning that the police discovered where she lived and phoned me to collect her from the hospital. There she sat happily chatting with a social worker, delighted with the valentine that someone had pinned on her and oblivious to the enormity of the situation. Our wonderful family doctor mobilized a geriatric assessment team and the diagnosis of dementia was finally made and plans put into place. The love that our family always had for Mom would need to sustain us as her dementia progressed, and guide us to find the right way. But it would take much more than that. Mom's view of the world had shifted and we were going to have to muster all our strength to understand what she was experiencing in order to honor and accept her for who she was–she deserved no less. The sadness was overwhelming as I realized that I was saying goodbye to the Mom that I knew and already grieving her loss. She had always stood by me through ups and downs and now it was my turn.

Dementia is a relentless disease that deprives a person of so much of who they are. On the other hand, knowing and loving a person allows you to still see and celebrate the remaining qualities and helps to sustain you through the gradual loss. My very well-brought-up mother who could be feisty and stand up for herself, but who was never rude, became paranoid as she began to forget familiar people. She started to believe that strangers were following her. Her behavior became aggressive and she was difficult to handle. I never had to collect my children from school or anywhere else for "bad behavior," but I did have to pick up my mother from her day program after she punched an ex-boxer in the nose. I found it heartbreaking when Mom could no longer recognize the pictures of her grandchildren and began smashing them. She thought that these unknown children would destroy her home. Starting the vacuum at the family cottage that summer threw her into a rage over perceived destruction, prompting her to hit me with a broom and run away into the woods. Despite the aggression, however, the feisty mom peeked through and I knew that she was still with me as long as she could fight back.

I always loved and appreciated my mother's excellent social skills, and even as the dementia accelerated, fragments of those social graces survived. Mom didn't consistently recognize my father and thought that two men lived in her apartment–Dad and the other unnamed man. Most of the time she remained civil to both of them. At Christmas we had a problem, though–both men needed Christmas presents! I had long since understood that there was no point in opposing her thinking and that I needed to play along. Dad received two presents from Mom that year and was under strict orders to play his part. Mom eventually could not recognize herself either and thought that another woman from her apartment building was following her. One day on the way into the hairdresser she caught sight of herself in the many mirrors and became quite annoyed that the "other woman" was behind her. However, as we left the salon, she told me that she wasn't happy about being followed but as "that woman" came from the same building we should at least offer her a ride home. I assured her that she was being very courteous, but the lady was still under the dryer and not ready to leave. Eventually we had to cover all the mirrors in their apartment to reduce Mom's fear of the "strangers."

Even as her memory and other faculties declined, Mom's joy in being with and working with other people persisted. For many years my immediate family has spent Thanksgiving at our cabin that my husband and I built north of Toronto. This particular year our household also included my mom and dad and mother-in-law. As usual, we all had our jobs preparing for Thanksgiving dinner and Mom eagerly participated with everyone else, peeling potatoes and just feeling happy to be in the group. Later in the week she told me that she had been away and didn't know who the ladies were or where she had been but it must have been a church kitchen because they all had worked together. She had had a wonderful time! To know that she could still experience such happiness was a joy to me.

The time came when we could no longer manage Mom in her home and the wrenching decision had to be made to place her in a secure unit of a nursing home. She needed constant supervision including throughout the night and that, together with her frequent bouts of aggression, were exhausting. I had always worked on the premise that despite her disease and difficult behavior, Mom deserved respect and loving care. I made many visits to prospective nursing homes looking for the one that could best nurture her and give her that respect as her faculties continued to decline. Many questions had to be addressed. How to make sure that she could still interact with people as she loved to before the dementia? How to provide creative outlets that even in her darkest moments and less aware state still gave her a sense of worth? How to make sure that the family who still loved her dearly could stay a part of her life? When the opportunity finally came and we moved her, leaving her behind for the first time, Dad and I were overwhelmed with sadness. We knew we were right in our decision, but it seemed unimaginable to leave the Mom that I loved alone.

As it turned out Mom did receive wonderful care and nurturing and the nursing home staff always welcomed us when we came to see her. I took Mom for long walks in her wheelchair and as we strolled along the lake shore, memory fragments surfaced now and again–sailing with her brother as a child and thoughts of her sister while watching the waves. She tried her best with "crafts," happy, but a shadow of her former talent. She loved the music programs and would sing along as best she could. We spent time drinking tea and just being content together. The long and very difficult journey that we had taken together was the expression of my love for her and was now reciprocated in her warm smiles. That is what kept me going through this painful time. To be able to spend these moments with her, to see her smile creep across her face as she slowly recognized me, to see the love in her eyes; all this was a most wonderful gift. Love sustained us both to the end.

"We had come this far; we wouldn't ruin it all now."

# What Is Space?

It was two o'clock in the morning. I was sleeping in my bed, my head comfortably sunk into my pillow, when I suddenly felt a small hand repeatedly tapping on my cheek. Then I heard a determined little voice.

"Maman, Maman, wake up, wake up. It's important. What is SPACE?"

Was I dreaming? I opened one eye and saw my four-year-old bundle of love in his red cotton pajamas, all excited, and waiting for an answer, urging me to get up; so I did.

We went to the kitchen and sat at the breakfast table. I was very sleepy, but Alistair's sparkling gaze sure woke me up fast.

"Maman, what is space?" he asked again.

He put his little chin inside his hands and his elbows on the table. I looked at him, totally in love with him, totally amazed and in awe in front of this little boy who so early in the morning had such existential questions.

I tried my best to answer in a simple way.

"Well, space is what you see when you look up to the sky, with the sun, and the moon and the stars."

He stared up at me, with a quizzical look on his face; then spoke in a solemn tone of voice.

"What is behind space?" he asked.

Now I had to think more seriously. "Well, there is more space, space that you cannot see."

"How do you get there?" Alistair asked with the same determination and gravity.

Wow! I was getting into deep trouble here. I tried to remain simple in my half-awake-half-asleep condition; however, I wanted to give him a true answer.

"You can go there with an airplane, then with a spaceship," I replied.

Alistair did not seem satisfied. He appeared deep in thought before speaking.

"No, no, no," he said. "You get there with IMAGINATION."

I felt more in awe. My four-year-old son had succeeded in encapsulating thousands and thousands of philosophical and metaphysical thoughts into one simple sentence – "...with imagination." By now I was totally awake and totally dazzled. I played his game

"Where is Imagination?" I asked. I thought he would answer me, "In my head."

Instead, he replied, with the simplest composure.

"In my heart."

I kissed him so hard and told him he was my precious little philosopher. I knew that de Saint-Exupéry's *The Little Prince* indeed existed.

# The Secret

It began like any other Easter Sunday morning. The obligatory chocolate eggs had been exchanged and subsequently devoured. It was a beautifully crisp day with barely a cloud in the sky, a perfectly ordinary day, by all accounts. My bedroom, suitably decorated in teenage fasion, was bathed in glaring sunlight as I perused the morning paper. My sister was reapplying her makeup in the bathroom next door while my brother was absorbed in the latest Play Station game in his room. My parents were in the kitchen enjoying their latest cup of coffee. Then the phone call came that turned this perfectly unspectacular Sunday into one of the most spectacular.

My mother, Aideen, her twin, Lorna, and their eldest sister, Enda are used to loss and the suffering that goes with it. The twins had been twelve and Enda fifteen when they were orphaned. Their beloved mother had died from a brain hemorrhage after being struck by a car as she cycled home from work. Their father had died six years earlier from a heart attack. Nine-year old Enda had been in the room when he collapsed. In a cruel twist, he had fallen against the door, preventing the frantic child from getting out and impeding those that came to help from getting in.

Following their mother's untimely death, they were left in the care of their Aunt Mary, who lived around the corner with a family of her own. They watched as relatives plundered their home of all their parent's possessions, including their father's beloved saxophone, which to this day cannot be found. Only the house itself was left untouched. The twins could legally claim it when they turned eighteen. Not even a single photograph of either parent was left to them.

At the age of nineteen, Enda was sent by my Grandaunt Mary to one of Ireland's infamous Magdalene laundries after becoming pregnant with her daughter Kate. These laundries, which were run by nuns, are synonymous with cruelty, abuse and pain. The young single mothers were made to scrub floors, do laundry and serve meals right up until the moment of birth. She stayed in that home for a nearly a year and a half until my mother could get her hands on their childhood home. Enda has never forgiven Grandaunt Mary for what she went through there and to this day refuses to be in her company.

My Aunt Lorna's late teenage years are equally as bleak. By age seventeen she was also pregnant and had fallen into the clutches of an abusive husband from whom she wouldn't escape for over a decade. My own parents only found out about the beatings when he nearly beat her to a pulp one night. Of the three siblings, my mother, known affectionately as Daydee, was the lucky one. She met my father at the age of fifteen and they have been together ever since. For me, they are the definition of soul mates. They still act like love-struck teenagers. My father had just turned nineteen while my mother was twenty when they married in June 1987. I was three months old at the time.

It was my Aunt Lorna who rang that Easter Sunday morning back in 2003.

"You are not going to believe what I'm about to tell you, Daydee," she said. "Mary is on the way to my house. We have a stepbrother we never knew about. Mammy gave him up in the fifties."

I will never forget the moment I was told. My father tapped lightly on my bedroom door.

"Can I come in, Bec?" he asked.

He opened the door and I knew the instant I looked at him that something serious had happened. My father is a strong man, both physically and mentally. He's not one for being overly emotional. He had this pained look on his face. Disbelief was pouring from every feature.

"You're mother has just been told she has a brother. She's just after getting off the phone with Lorna."

In that moment, it felt like time had stopped. As I stood there, completely overwhelmed, it felt like everything around me became blurred and distorted. My father was saying something else but I didn't hear him. At the age of sixteen, I was beginning to learn what my mother and aunts had gone through and this latest revelation felt like a slap in the face. I had never seen my father so unnerved. He didn't linger long before returning to my mother's side.

I didn't immediately rush down to my mother. I just sat on my bed completely at a loss. A thousand thoughts rushed through my head but one kept returning. Why had they never been told?

An hour later, Aunt Lorna arrived. She went straight to the kitchen. Through the door I could hear their muffled conversation. Lorna stayed until it began to get dark. Once I heard her leave, I took a deep breath and made my way downstairs. My mother sat in the corner of the kitchen. She was pale and her face appeared empty and withdrawn. She appeared tired, as if the weight of the world had just been put on her shoulders. I stood there in silence for what felt like an eternity before my father spoke.

Grandaunt Mary had given Lorna only a few details about this lost brother. Their mother, Kathleen, had given birth to James Christopher Brien on December 15, 1956 in Southampton, England. She had fled Ireland with the boy's father, Ducker, shortly after realizing she was pregnant. Ireland in the 1950s was a cruel, harsh place for unmarried mothers. They were seen as the worst of sinners, ostracized by their families, the State and of course, the Church. Kathleen's mother was a particularly harsh woman and staunchly religious to boot. The reason they had sought refuge in Southampton was because Ducker's sister Margaret lived there. The young couple stayed there until the baby was seven months old. Here the story gets a little murky. Kathleen and Ducker's relationship ended shortly afterwards. We still don't know what happened between them. It's a case of the rest of the family not knowing or they were simply not willing to talk about it. I feel the latter is true. My mother's family is full of staunch believers that what happens in the past stays there.

Indeed, Ducker's sister Margaret is the only reason we ever found out about this baby boy. It had been her brother's dying wish for her to find James. On his deathbed he had called her to his side and whispered, "Find my boy. Find me and Kathleen's boy."

The news of her search quickly made its way to Grandaunt Mary. At the time, Mary was neighbors with a relative of Duckers who had spilt the beans. They had become very close friends over the years and as soon as Margaret had told the rest of the family of her plans, Grandaunt Mary was on the phone to my Aunt Lorna.

On that Easter Sunday evening in 2003 and in the immediate days that followed, an eerie silence descended upon our house. Our home has never been quiet. People are always coming and going. It's a home full of laughter and storytelling, but this revelation had shocked us all into an unnerving disquiet made up of disbelief, grief and anger. My mother barely spoke until Enda arrived home four days later. It was only years later that my father told me that in those few days my mother had reverted to her sixteen-year-old self–sad, withdrawn, lonely and worryingly quiet.

Enda's return brought another revelation. In the days following their mother's funeral, a neighbor had told the sisters that Kathleen had given birth to their stepbrother a number of years before she met their father, Jim. Enda had been born to my grandparents on February 2, 1963, while my mother and Aunt Lorna followed on December 21st 1966, over a decade after their stepbrother had been born. Enda went to Grandaunt Mary about this baby boy, but Mary had dismissed it as the blatherings of a crazy old neighbor woman.

With Enda now home, a plan materialized. There was no time wasted asking any of their aunts and uncles who had kept this secret from them. They went straight to Ducker's sister, Margaret. She was returning home to Ireland that very weekend to begin her own search for James. My mother and aunts met with Margaret exactly a week after first being told about this baby boy. She told them all she knew.

In August 1957, Kathleen and Ducker had returned to Ireland in the hope of starting a new life together with their son. Despite still being shunned by her family, Kathleen moved into a house with Ducker on the edge of town. By Margaret's account, they seemed like a perfectly happy young family, but a month later, Ducker was on a boat back to England and my grandmother was left with a small baby with no way to support him, no family to help, no Church to run to and no State aid. Two weeks later, she had given him up for adoption and was back living with her family, all forgiven, all forgotten.

She had taken James to Sean Ross Abbey, a church-run institution for unwed mothers, which was located in the town next to ours. In 2003, the home had been long closed. A chapel in ruins, choked with ivy, and a small graveyard, overgrown and unkempt beside it, greeted my mother and aunts when they made the journey there the day after meeting Margaret. Even now, my Aunt Lorna sometimes makes the short journey there. What she's looking for only she knows. A quick Internet search later that evening revealed that the headquarters of the former institution was now based in County Cork, over three hours away. A phone call was made, their situation explained and a meeting was set up for a week later with the nun in charge of the adoption files.

Those seven days were the toughest I have ever experienced in my house. My parents and I, along with my brother and sister, are incredibly close. We talk a lot and are quick to laugh and joke around. We are fiercely protective of each other, and ours is a tightly-knit group that is not easily compromised. But during this time, we barely spoke a word to each other. There was no easy laughter, no conversation on any topic. I think we just didn't know what to say. The unrelenting silence, coupled with the anguished look on my mother's face, was hard to bear. I have always idolized my mother. She is beautiful, caring, giving and honest and would do anything for me. She's the best mother anyone could hope for. Watching her suffer like that made me incredibly angry. At sixteen, I knew very little about my mother's side of the family. She never spoke about them, never interacted with them. To this day, I'm still angry about the whole episode.

The day dawned for mother and Aunt Lorna's long journey to Cork. Enda had returned to London a few days before due to work commitments. It was a grey, bleak day. They arrived at their destination, Bessborough Estate, shortly after 11 a.m. The imposing three-storey Georgian mansion was as grey as the day. Its façade was imposing, even threatening. Its many windows were dressed in a white light muslin, concealing the many secrets that lay behind them. Sister Sarto greeted them at the door. The elderly nun was in charge of the adoption files. After introducing herself to them, she explained that she had met many families in their predicament.

She ushered them into her office, an old estate room filled with a large desk and other non-descript pieces of brown furniture. Piles and piles of folders and files smothered her desk. She took her seat behind it and my mother and aunt followed her lead, sitting directly opposite her. She took up a cream colored folder from the top of the pile at her right hand, opened the folder and began flicking through the pages.

"Now ladies, as I am sure you are well aware, under law, I cannot give you your stepbrother's adoption file," she said. "All I can tell you is that he was indeed cared for at Sean Ross Abbey from September 1957. He was given the best of care by the sisters there and did not need for

244

anything. He was…" She was interrupted by a soft knock on the door.

"Enter," Sister Sarto called.

A short nun, with graying brown hair and a kindly face appeared from behind the heavy oak door.

"Sorry to interrupt Sister, but there is an urgent phone call for you at the reception desk. I think you should take it," she said apologetically, her face reddening as she spoke.

"Excuse me ladies. I will deal with this and be with you momentarily," Sister Sarto said sharply. She made her way out of the room leaving the door slightly ajar.

My Aunt Lorna walked to the door and carefully peeped out to see where they had gone. The two nuns were down the corridor. Sister Sarto was talking on the phone while the other sister was looking on with a worried look painted on her face. Lorna made her way back to the desk.

"Okay Daydee, you keep an eye on the door and I'll have a look through this file."

My mother walked gingerly to the door, her eyes fixed on the back of Sister Sarto's head while Lorna reached over the desk and grabbed the file. The first page contained nothing of interest, just the child's name, mother's name and the date he had arrived at Sean Ross Abbey. The next few pages contained things like his weight, any illnesses he had, eye color, hair color, their mother's details, address, age, etc.

"Well, Lorna?" my mother called from the door.

"There's nothing here about where he was adopted to," she said anxiously. She rifled through the pages, frantically looking for where he had gone.

"Lorna, hurry," my mother said. "Sister Sarto is just after hanging up the phone."

"I'm trying." Lorna called. "This bloody file is all over the place."

Sister Sarto said something to another nun before turning on her heel and making her way back to the room.

"Lorna, she's coming back, quick, quick!"

Lorna nearly ripped some of the pages as she turned them. Just as Sister Sarto's footsteps were audible from the corridor, Lorna's eyes fell upon what she needed: adoptive parents and place of adoption.

"I've got it, I've got," she almost shouted.

My mother ran back to her seat while Lorna quickly replaced the file on the nun's desk. Just as she was sitting down in her chair, Sister Sarto reappeared through the door.

"I'm so sorry about that, ladies," she said, clearly annoyed. She placed herself back in her chair. "Now, where were we?" she said, "Oh, yes, your stepbrother's adoption file. The only person who has the right to this is the man himself. I'm afraid the only way you're going to find him is if he comes looking for you.'"

"Is there nothing else we can do, Sister?" my mother asked.

"'I'm afraid not, my dear. The law on this is very clear. I appreciate you have made a long journey here today but there is nothing else I can do for you. Can I perhaps get you a cup of tea or coffee?"

"No thank you, sister," Aunt Lorna replied. "We do have a long journey ahead of us so I think we really should be on our way. Thank you for taking the time to see us. We do really appreciate it."

As Sister Sarto closed the door on them, my mother and Lorna walked slowly down the steps and made their way back to the car.

"Well?" my mother asked as Lorna started the engine, "What did you find out?"

Lorna turned to my mother. She had a wicked glint in her eye.

"I got exactly what we need to find him. His adoptive parents' names and where he went."

"And are you going to share this information?" my mother said jokingly.

The twins laughed for the first time in over two weeks.

"He was adopted by a young Irish couple, Augustus and Brigid Hennelly, from county Mayo. But he didn't move to County Mayo. Oh no, he was sent across the Atlantic Ocean to Chicago in the U.S of A."

The twins spent the rest of the journey wondering what had become of this baby boy, what kind of life he'd had, what his parents were like and if he looked like them.

That night they called Enda in London and told her of their exploits in Cork. She said she would take the search from there. She enlisted the help of a private investigator in the English capital. A few days passed and there was still no sign of James Hennelly. Searches of ancestry sites, voting registers and newspaper articles had proved fruitless. Everyone was beginning to become frustrated and my mother and Aunt Lorna were clearly exhausted from what had happened in the last couple of weeks. I was beginning to get sick of the whole thing myself. I just wanted everything to return to normal. Things like this only happened in films or books. I wanted my mother back, but I knew she and my aunts would not rest until they found this man.

Enda flew back to Ireland, three weeks to the day that they had first learned of their stepbrother. They were all sitting in Lorna's house that Sunday evening, looking through more ancestry sites. Lorna's house had become the base of their investigation in recent weeks, which meant I saw very little of my mother. She worked during the day while I attended school, and in the evenings, she and my father would be at Lorna's trying to decide on the next step of their search. It was past 11 o'clock that night. They had all taken a coffee break after hours of trawling through different sites. My mother, Lorna, Enda and my father were sitting around the kitchen table, when Enda had a moment of inspiration.

"We never checked the bloody Chicago phone book for him, did we?" she said. "It's so bloody obvious! Why didn't I think of it before?"

They all left their latest cups of coffee untouched as they crowded around the computer screen one more time. Five minutes later, there were three James Hennellys before their eyes in Chicago.

"The only thing to do is ring all three," my mother said.

"I'll do it," Enda said, "I'm the eldest!" She picked up the handset and dialed. It rang and rang and rang. "It's gone to a message machine," Enda said. "Probably not a good idea to leave the poor guy a message. We can try it again later."

Excitement was quickly replaced by disappointment as she prepared to dial the second number. The tension in the air was rising with every passing second. James Hennelly number two answered the phone on the second ring.

"Could I speak to James Hennelly, please," Enda asked clearly.

"This is James Hennelly. How can I help you?" he replied.

"This is going to sound very strange, but my name is Enda and I am looking for my brother. We believe he was adopted from Ireland to Chicago in the late 1950s and his name is James Hennelly. His adoptive parents are Augustus and Brigid.

You wouldn't be him by any chance, would you?"

There was a deafening silence for about five seconds. The others looked on with eyes as big as saucers before James Hennelly number two calmly replied.

"I am very sorry, but I am not the man you are looking for. I was born here in Chicago in the late sixties to my parents, Tom and Annie."

Enda's face went from hope to despair in an instant, and the others knew straight away he wasn't who they were looking for.

"I see,' Enda managed to say. "Thank you for taking my call. I know it's probably one of the strangest calls you will ever get."

"That's no problem at all,' he replied. "All the best in your search. I hope you find him."

"Thank you very much," Enda replied. "Goodbye." Third time lucky, I suppose," she said to the others as she dialed the last number. It rang and rang and rang. Enda was just about to hang up when a man answered.

"Can I speak to James Hennelly, please," she asked again.

"Speaking," came the response from James Hennelly number three.

She repeated exactly what she said to James number two. She could hear the phone being dropped at the end of the line. It went quiet for about ten seconds.

"What's happening?" asked my Aunt Lorna.

"I think he dropped the phone. All I can hear is muffled voices," Enda replied. Lorna was about to say something before Enda silenced her.

"Hello, Enda." An elderly man had picked up the phone. "This is Jim's father, Gus. He is the James you are looking for. You'll forgive my son. He's clearly shaken by the news."

"Can you give me a second please, Gus," Enda responded. She closed her eyes for a moment. "It's him." she said calmly. "It's him. We found him."

"Thank God," Lorna said.

My mother didn't say a word. She just sat there, calm and collected, knowing deep in her heart that they would have found him no matter what.

Enda spoke to Gus for over an hour. He told her all about Jim Hennelly. He had come to them at the age of two along with an Irish girl, Mary. He was a police officer in the Cook County Police Department and had been married the year before at the age of forty-six. Gus had told Jim, at the age of twelve, that he had been adopted from Ireland. He said the young man had never shown any signs of interest in looking for his birth parents. Gus also ensured Enda that he had a wonderful life growing up, that he never wanted for anything and that his birth parents would be relieved to know that he had a good life.

"Unfortunately, they are no longer with us, Gus," Enda replied. "Our mother died a long time ago in 1978."

"I am very sad to hear that, Enda. Jim will be too. How about you guys give us a call back tomorrow at the same time? I'm sure Jim will be more than happy to speak to you."

"Yes, Gus, we'll do that; goodbye for now," Enda said before replacing the handset.

Jim was more than happy to speak to his Irish stepsisters. The next day he told us that he was distraught that his birth mother had died, but he was very excited to gain three new sisters. Enda, Lorna and my mother all took turns speaking to their new sibling. It was the phone call that changed everything. The mother that left our house

253

earlier that Monday evening never came back. The woman that returned was the mother I knew and loved. It was my mother who was quick to smile and laugh. Gone was the withdrawn, heartbroken woman who had been lied to for most of her life by the people who were supposed to protect and help her.

It had taken the three sisters just three weeks to find Jim and indeed three months later, my mother and Aunt Lorna boarded a plan to Chicago to meet the man himself. For me, my dad and my siblings, it was the longest ten days of our lives but for my mother they were some of her happiest. She would call us each night, telling us about what they had done and where they had gone that day. The first night they arrived they had been whisked to a big family party and introduced to each member of the extended Hennelly clan.

"We are being treated like celebrities here, Bec," my mother told me one night. "Everyone wants to meet us and get a picture with us."

She told me how much he looked like them. He had indeed inherited the Brien genes. His hair had turned white in his mid-twenties, just like my mother and some of her aunts and uncles. I myself am also experiencing the white hair gene at the age of twenty-four. When she showed us photos of him a few weeks later, it was uncanny how much Jim looked like his sisters. It was the eyes mostly, those clear bright, blue eyes.

My mother and aunt were treated to everything Chicago had to offer, a cruise along the Lakeshore one day, a trip up the Sears Tower another, shopping on Millionaire Mile, and a walk through Navy Pier the next. She explained how they had slept like babies each night because they had done so much during the day.

When my mother finally returned to us, she just glowed with happiness. She had this brightness in her eyes. Months later I asked her what was her favorite part of her trip to Chicago.

"Jim always wanted to be close to us, whether it was sitting next to us at dinner or walking along Navy Pier," she replied. "He's a good man that our mother would be proud of."

Up until that moment, my mother had never spoken about her mother to me. I think it's a mixture of things. I bear a striking resemblance to my grandmother. I don't think my mother had ever fully recovered from her mother's death. Meeting her brother, Jim, happened over twenty-five years after her mother had died. That death had opened up a wound for my mother that only meeting Jim could somehow heal.

A year later it was Jim's turn to make the long journey home across the Atlantic Ocean. He came with his wife. We were all waiting patiently outside our house for their rental car to appear. When they finally arrived, I was shocked when this tall, powerful-looking man with white hair emerged. I had seen pictures of him, of course, but to see him firsthand and to behold how much he looked like my mother and her sisters took my breath away. My mother and aunts were as proud as Cheshire cats as they introduced him to his new Irish family. We were all in awe of him, and we all loved him instantly. It felt like he had always been a part of the family. The ease with which he, my mother and aunts interacted brought a smile to everyone's face, including mine. Up until that point, I had never seen my mother so happy.

While he was home, he made the journey to Cork where he was given his adoption file. Contained within it was a letter my grandmother had written to her baby boy. She explained that she had made a mistake in giving him up, that she loved him more than anything in the world and would be back to get him in a couple of days. She did return to get him but the nuns told her he had already been adopted when in fact he didn't leave that home until he was two years of age. A cruel twist but, at least, Jim knew that she loved him even if they were callously separated.

It's only now when I look back at this time, that I realize how powerful love is. It doesn't matter if a mother and her daughters are separated by death or for how long. I truly believe my mother and sisters would have gone to the ends of this earth to find their stepbrother. To this day, their love for their mother is so palpable it doesn't feel like she died nearly thirty-four years ago. I understand this love because it's the same love my mother has for me and I have for her.

*This story is dedicated to the grandmother I never met, Kathleen, and to her short but important life.*

Rebecca Kelly

# I Love You, Dad

As I look at his picture my thoughts turn to my dad. He passed away more than a decade ago at the age of 89. Dad was born in a village in Poland, the son of poor peasants who made their living peddling household goods. His home, as a boy, was a shack with a dirt floor. He shared this humble space with his mom and three sisters while his dad was over here working to save the money to bring his family to a better life. Hunger was dad's constant companion during those years. Root vegetables were the bulk of his diet with a bit of chicken on special occasions. For dad, wasting food was a sin. Giving food, even tinned or packaged, was his way of showing love.

My grandfather brought his family over here when my dad was eight. Dad went through the school system, then on to university and law school. After graduation he set up practice and met and married Mom. My two sisters and I soon came along. He was living a life almost unimaginable to the poor boy in Poland.\While Dad loved his family, he had developed other passions, one was golf and the other was fishing. He was an avid fisherman, deep-sea fishing in winter and heading north for muskies, pike and pickerel in the summer. I have many happy memories of sitting with him in a boat on a still lake waiting for the perch to bite. Blueberry pie and a tall glass of milk at some small town diner was often the perfect end for those idyllic days.

I particularly remember one cold and snowy January morning when my sisters and I were teenagers. Dad had left the house well before dawn dressed in his warmest fishing clothes while the rest of us slept soundly under our quilts. When he arrived at the lake he chopped a hole in the ice, lowered his line and sat patiently on his little stool waiting for the smelt to bite.

A few hours later, when the sun had risen to give us a gloriously bright day, Dad returned home with quite a catch. We, of course, were still asleep. He gutted and scaled a big mess of smelt, seasoned and dredged them in flour and dropped them into hot oil in the frying pan. While that was happening, he also threw some buns in the oven to warm, set the table, put on the kettle and cut up a platter's worth of fresh vegetables.

When all was ready Dad walked over to the stereo and picked out one of his favorite records, Scottish bagpipe music. He turned the volume up as high as it would go and let the sound do its magic. From deep under the sheets I poked my head out when I heard, "And here come the McGregors!" just before the drone of the pipes began.

One by one, my sisters, Mom and I staggered out of our beds to find out what all the racket was about. On the dining room table was a mouth-watering feast. There was nothing quite so wonderful as this fish fry breakfast, my father's delicious and eloquent expression of his feelings for us.

I love you, Dad.

# Part Three

# Tails of Love

# Wilbur

One evening about twenty months ago, my son, who is a young man and not quite flown the nest, came to me asking if he could get a dog. As we already had three cats living with us at the time and all belonging to my son, I said no. "But, Mom, I promise I will do everything," said my son to this most gullible of women. "You won't have to do a thing."

After much brow beating I relented and said yes. It didn't take more than 24 hours for my son to come home with Wilbur, a little Dachshund puppy with floppy ears, a silky coat, one blue eye and one brown. He was adorable. We made a home for him in the kitchen, and that was the beginning of a HUGE shock for me. There started to appear animal droppings everywhere in the kitchen. Heaven forbid Wilbur got upstairs to the bedrooms where he'd do his doggy best to mark his territory!

Now, to be fair, Wilbur has always been the sweetest of puppies. He is loving

and good-natured. He's also one smart dog.
Wilbur loves to play and go on walks. My
son says he's a chick magnate. I can see that
this might be so as all kinds of people stop
to say hello to Wilbur.

I love Wilbur, I really do, but there is
one big challenge with this little fellow.
Wilbur is a chewer. He started with the
pedestal of my Duncan Phyfe mahogany
dining table, worked his way through part of
the kitchen door and the frame of the
backyard doors. He also chewed through the
upholstery and down to the stuffing on the
kitchen banquette. He seemed to relish
working away on my brand new Ecco shoe,
but the cause of his fame and notoriety has
been the work his did on my passport the
night before I was to fly to Mexico for a
holiday. When I realized that the passport I
had been frantically looking for had fallen
out of my back pocket and was now in
Wilbur's paws I quickly grabbed it away. He
had chewed it in the corners but, fortunately,
the photo and all the print were fine. I didn't
think there would be any problem and went
to bed anticipating being in Mexico the
following day. Wrong.

When I got the airport the next
morning I was told by the Air Canada
personnel that there was no way I was going

to Mexico with my chewed passport. "Mexico will send you back," they said. I needed to get a new passport they advised. I was in shock.

It was possible to get a passport in one business day, expensive, but possible. I needed to go into downtown Toronto to the passport office. I checked my bags at the airport and attempted to rebook my flight for the next day. "There are no available seats on that flight," said the Air Canada employee behind the counter. I started to cry. "Let me just check with my boss," she said. She did that and, lo and behold, a seat became available.

I went back into the city in my snow boots and light spring jacket. It was well below freezing. When I got to the passport office I was told that, even though I had a passport, I would have to go through the whole application process again. "Oh, no!" I cried. Off I went on a marathon of having my picture taken, finding three people to sign and vouch for me and needing to get back to the passport office with all of that plus my birth certificate by 2:30 if it was to be processed that day. No birth certificate! I couldn't find it anywhere.

I returned to the passport office hoping what I had with me was good enough. No dice. I cried. A nice young man who worked there handed me a box of tissues, reassuring me that everything would be all right. "Go to the nearby Staples Business Depot and apply for a birth certificate online. We will accept that."

Off I sped only to find the only customer computer in Staples occupied. I waited and waited and finally begged the occupant to let me go on. "I'm busy," came the impatient reply.

I raced to another Staples store several blocks away. A kind young employee helped me through the whole application process and wouldn't charge me. She is a saint. Grasping my receipt in my hand, I hailed a cab and got back to the passport office just as my time was running out. Everything after that ran smoothly and by 4:30 I had my new temporary passport in my hands. That day had cost me $400, and I was now several years older than I had been the day before.

The next morning I went back to the airport and the start of a wonderful Mexican holiday, but not before saying good bye, with a hug and a kiss, to Wilbur, sweet, sweet Wilbur (alias Wilbur, the Devil Dog).

# Bonito

My husband Harold and I were in northern Germany one winter while I studied dressage in Verden, near Hanover. Hanover is the center for the Hanoverian breed of horse and the location of the Hanoverian auction in April. For three weeks I attended the preliminaries where they train the young horses for the auction. Harold showed up and wanted to bid on a horse named Bonito that I hadn't tried and knew nothing about. Harold investigated by talking to several people. A man from Colorado told Harold that the horse was fabulous and to go for it. Only three people had tried the horse during the preliminaries and he was a little-known contender.

The gala auction evening arrived. Swags of flowers filled the candle-lit arena. Everyone wore black tie, and the champagne flowed freely to loosen up the bidding. The auction started. Number 44, Bonito, trotted out and Harold started bidding on him. Bonito was a magnificent Hanoverian dressage horse. I had said what my limit was but when the bidding reached it, however, a couple of people in our crowd kept punching me and telling me to keep going. We bid a couple more times and we bought the horse.

That night, after the auction, we went to meet him. When I entered his stall, he gave me a big slurpy kiss, starting with his tongue at the bottom of my neck all the way up my face, and then he did the same thing to Harold.

"I told you," Harold said. "This is it."

The next day I rode him and I thought he was fabulous. It seemed like riding on a cloud or on springs. He was just a dancer who liked to show off. He loved it when people watched and applauded.

We made arrangements to ship him to our California home. When he arrived, we took him out of the trailer and turned him into an arena so he could run around and get the kinks out of his legs after his long trip. He immediately started galloping, bucking and careening around the arena. Then he flew over the high fence and galloped next door to visit some cows in the field. We caught him and put him back into the arena but he made a return visit to the cows. I thought, *Oh my goodness! This horse must have grown up on a farm in Germany and he was just saying hi to the neighborhood.*

When in California we moved to another farm owned by a friend of mine. She had a pygmy goat named Michaela, a precious little nanny goat that came up to Bonito's knee. When Bonito arrived at the farm, Michaela checked him out and decided he was the one she wanted to live with, so she picked him out of the twelve horses already there and moved into the stall with him.

Every morning Bonito bathed Michaela with his tongue, licking her all over and cleaning her up. Then they shared breakfast. At night she snuggled up and they slept together. When I came down to ride she was not happy to see me. At first she tried to keep me out of the stall. She butted me a couple of times before letting me take Bonito out. I saddled him and began to head him out towards the arena, and there we met Michaela with her feet straddled out, giving me a cold stare as if saying, "You are not taking my boyfriend."

I diverted her with a little grain but once she finished eating, she again tried to intercept. She ran in front of Bonito and he screeched to a halt to avoid hurting her. I had no choice but to get someone to come for Michaela and tie her up. That was Bonito's first experience with a little animal.

I started riding Bonito and showing him. He was a real champion with tremendous presence. He loved to show off and swelled up and danced around the arena. We obtained many good scores and a championship. He grew in experience and I enjoyed him so much.

Later in his life, we decided to move to Mexico. We bought a ranch and brought Bonito with us. We turned him out into the fields and he was as happy as he could be. He was always adventuresome and curious and loved every place that he went.

Soon after our arrival in Mexico, someone dumped an orphan lamb onto our property. Early one morning when I went out to the stable, I heard this kitten-like mewing. I looked all around and saw a tiny lamb that was so weak he could hardly stand. I sent the stable boy down to the closest grocery store, which was near the highway in a little village. He returned with a baby bottle and some milk. We started feeding the lamb and we fed him for about six weeks till he could eat on his own. After that, the lamb made himself quite at home.

As was his custom, he made friends with all the animals, including the cats and the dogs. We named him Lambie.

Bonito and Lambie checked each other out. He moved into the stall with Bonito. Lambie could go in and out, but he liked to spend his days with Bonito. Bonito was a huge horse and ate a lot. So did Lambie. He began to grow. He got bigger and bigger and fatter and fatter. Finally, we had to separate them because we were afraid that Lambie would bloat because he ate so much trying to keep up with Bonito. Sadly, we had to take him out of Bonito's stall. We were given another orphan, this time a goat. We kept the goat in with Lambie so that Lambie wouldn't be too lonely, but Lambie always missed Bonito. Every chance he had to get out of his coral he would run to see Bonito.

One day my husband took some guests at the ranch out to the stable to show them the horses. As my husband strolled out, Bonito, whom we allowed to roam free, came up to Harold, put his head on Harold's shoulder and basically said to him, "I'm sick."

Harold looked at Bonito and noticed he was sweating. He knew that something was terribly wrong. We called the vet.

Bonito was very sick. He had a severe case of colic. We treated him for about twenty-four hours. The vet stayed with him the whole time. At five o'clock in the morning the vet gave me his prognosis.

"We have to take him to Mexico City if we're going to save him," he said. "He's going to have to have surgery and there are no facilities here."

Mexico City was about five hours away. There was a very good chance that the police would stop us. Taking a horse into Mexico City, especially during weekdays, is very risky. The police like to stop people, impound the car and trailer and charge a big fine for not having the correct papers to bring an animal in. On top of that, we had foreign licenses on our vehicles. I was very nervous about the trip. The vet agreed to go with me. He knew the location of the university hospital for horses. This kind vet drove the truck and we took Bonito down at about 9 a.m.

We arrived at the vet school. The vets examined Bonito. He could hardly stand up and kept leaning on me. He was in terrible pain. They decided to go ahead and operate. Bonito survived the surgery. I spent a couple of nights there. University students watched him around the clock. I was very impressed by the attention they gave him. The vets felt that he was on the mend and he just needed his strength back to get on his feet and could probably go home in a couple of weeks, so I returned to our ranch.

I received emails from the vet who continued caring for him every day. Dr. Valasquez sent me pictures of Bonito. At first he felt very optimistic about Bonito's recovery. Then he called me. He said that Bonito had gone into a decline; he was very depressed and he would not eat. He kept dropping weight and had lost interest in living. His condition was serious and coming home would jeopardize his recovery.

"I just don't know what to do about him," Dr. Valasquez said. "He's pining away. We're trying to give him all the attention that we can, but he's just extremely depressed."

"I will definitely come down, and I will bring a friend of his," I said.

I called the local vet and asked him if he could come with me in the car to take Lambie. Lambie was now over a year old and enormous. He was not pleased with the prospect of a trip in the back of the SUV.

Off we went at 9 p.m., the time my vet thought we might have the best chance to drive an animal through Mexico City without the police stopping us. We had put cardboard on the floor at the back of the car. After riding for a couple of hours, Lambie became fed up with this whole journey and started butting the windows in the back of the SUV. We tried putting some of the cardboard on the windows but Lambie ate it. After this wild trip, we made it to Mexico City at about two in the morning. The city's night life was still going on and so traffic was heavy. As we drove through the middle of town, we created great interest in the other drivers and their passengers, especially when they could hear a loud "bah" in the back of the SUV. Some of these very sophisticated Mexicans kept peering into our car and wondering who these local yokels were. They seemed quite horrified.

We arrived at the vet school and I went into the stable to see Bonito. I walked into his stall and saw that he was absolutely emaciated. He could hardly lift his head to acknowledge me – rare, because I usually received the big slurp. I thought, *This truly is an emergency.*

We grabbed Lambie, opened the door to the stall and put him in with Bonito. Lambie ran around inside and rubbed up against Bonito's legs. Bonito began to come to. His eyes opened wide; he looked at Lambie and gave him a big slurp. Lambie ran to the corner of the stall into an enormous pile of hay that Bonito had been ignoring. Lambie began to gorge himself. Bonito turned around and also started eating. I had brought some carrots and he finished them.

I spent a couple of hours there early that morning and then I went to a hotel to get some sleep. When I came back, Bonito's head hung outside the stall window and he gave me a nice little nicker. I could tell right away that there was a change in Bonito's appetite and his whole attitude. He was so happy to have his buddy with him.

Every day I went to the university campus and took Bonito out for a walk because his therapy included getting a little exercise. Of course, Lambie came with me, trotting along behind. The students thought this was a riot. They kept calling Lambie *Barbeque*. The atmosphere was very relaxed and everybody felt so happy to see Bonito and Lambie. We became part of the campus routine.

After a couple of weeks, Bonito had recovered sufficiently that I felt it unnecessary for me to stay there. All the veterinary students, especially the women, had fallen madly in love with Bonito and Lambie. Bonito was never alone, so I knew he was well cared for. I returned to the ranch and about ten days later Dr. Valasquez told me that Bonito was ready to come home. I went down to get him.

Bonito had a long recovery at home. It took about six months before I could actually start riding him again. He was back to his old self and we had many musical performances where I would choreograph music to a piece of dressage that I had composed. We would perform for an event, which Bonito always loved because he loved showing off for people.

Unfortunately, Bonito died two years ago, but we still have Lambie. He turned out to be an enormous ram with huge curling horns. He's very spoiled and very privileged, but he has never found a buddy that he loves as much as he loved Bonito.

# Cats I Have Known

I wish I could remember the first day
First hour, first moment of your meeting me
So unrecorded did it slip away.

- Christina Rossetti

I remember the first moment I met all the significant cats in my life. Cats have always been part of my life. As a toe-headed toddler I smile from the family album holding a black kitty. At five years of age I am dressing my cat in doll's clothes and taking her for jaunts in my doll carriage. An only child for six years until my sister arrives, cats are my first companions. My father indulges me and I am allowed to carry my pet in a little basket on outings to the local country store where the kindly owner gives me candy treats.

As they are now, cats were playmates and friends when I grew up during the 1950s. We lived on a small hobby farm outside of Toronto so all our cats were "outdoor" cats.

One afternoon, my sister and I found a mother and three kittens abandoned on the roadside. This was common practice, thinking a farmer would take them in–it was and still is cruel. Would you dump a small child on the side of the road and expect it to fend for itself? Barn cats lead short lives filled with calamity. As I was looking for a kitten a few years back, a friend took me to a farm she knew. I couldn't believe the condition of some of the twenty-two animals there–eyes poked out, mange, mites, pieces of ear missing. Most were feral having never been handled as kittens. All seemed fearful.

"We feed our cats," the farmer proudly announced as he poured no-name puppy chow into a huge metal dish, as starving cats battled for position. "Most farmers expect them to survive on mousing alone."

But what of our charges? Being children we didn't know better and named the mother cat Stinky. She had diarrhea and died shortly. (Going to the vet's was not something that was done unless a cow was having a breach birth–that justified the expense.)

The three charming kittens were named according to their markings: Marmalade for the orange male, Pinafore for the little female with the white and grey markings and Tiger for the tiny tabby. The idea wasn't original. My mother had read us a British picture book titled *Marmalade and Pinafore*. Come to think of it, I came up with Tiger because of her stripes. You'd never name a person due to their looks or characteristics but it was common for animals. Imagine what T.S. Eliot's cats would think of that?

Tiger was the sweetest creature and the only cat my mother ever allowed in the house. Tiger slept in a doll bassinette by my bed, gently took potato chips out of my mother's mouth and had her first litter in our living room. To this day I can hear her loud cries and see her circling in confusion. I got a cardboard box and filled it with towels and stayed beside her petting and soothing her through the throes of birth. I was twelve and knew little of the world. The first kitten arrived. By instinct, Tiger bit the amniotic sack and began cleaning him. She proved an attentive and loving mother. She patiently nursed her babies and later taught them how to mouse. She asked little and gave much. People who think cats are independent and distant have not known a cat.

"I didn't know I liked cats, till I lived with one," said my boyfriend David.

Many cats came and went throughout my childhood, disappeared, died too soon. Little Tiger left an indelible imprint on my heart. She was my first pet. Mine. All mine. What stood out most besides her gentleness and loving ways was her coming and going from my life. My constant friend for four years was tragically taken from me. She died before my eyes one rainy Thursday. I was just sixteen. With the rain my mother had decided to drive us to school. As she backed out of the driveway, I saw Tiger's body writhing. In the rush, no one had checked under the car. Cats like warm, dry places near engines. My mother forced me to go to school that sad day. Later we buried Tiger in the garden.

I was thirty years old before the next cat entered my life. I mute commercials but watched "the toilet paper kitties" frolic in the cottony soft bathroom tissue. It made me long for a white Persian. Those felines were purebred Chinchilla Persians; years later I actually met their breeder at a cat show. Did the ad sell toilet paper or dreams? Have you ever noticed the number of fluffy kittens on birthday cards? I have amassed quite a collection over the years, all sent by well-meaning friends who refer to me as "a cat person."

I can't resist petting cute little dogs as I stroll the boardwalk in the Beach. In France, the French love me as I compliment them on their beaux petits chiens. But it's cats I relate to in lifestyle and personality. I like the yin and yang of cats. They can be playful, yet peaceful. They snuggle up; then need their space. They are easy pets for working people to care for, not requiring frequent walks. The litter box can be hidden; in fact, cats prefer discretion. They thrive on dry food and water, and have the good sense to eat only when actually hungry. Cats I have known, greet me joyously on arrival home. We are happy to see each other.

Am I the one doing the searching or do cats seek me out? How much destiny is involved? Buddhists believe that we get what we need. When I meet the right cat, the connection is instant. It's like that with people too.

One summer while visiting family in rural Ontario, David and I stopped at a roadside stand to buy fresh corn. David pointed out the sign *Free Kittens*. He'd heard me talking about wanting a kitten. With my country roots, I was not completely convinced that a cat could live happily in an apartment.

"Just take a look at him," said David.

The farmer emerged from a barn board back kitchen with a fluffy, wriggling bundle of dark brown and black striped fur, with tiny white feet, white tummy and blaze of white on his face. Being long haired, the kitten possessed a huge lion-like ruff.

"He's not white," I protested.

"Just hold him; he has lots of white fur," he said as he placed the kitten in my arms.

Living in a back shed, Muff had not been socialized but at eight weeks, time was on our side. Muff crawled all over the car. Once home he promptly hid under the fridge, surfacing only to eat. That's when I would pet him and speak softly to him. Soon he was joining us on the couch and fetching wine corks. We'd toss them across the living room. Muff would retrieve the cork, place it at our feet and meow for more fun.

I'm not sure why I named him Muffin. I do recall a carrot muffin bitten right through the saran wrap with big chunks missing. Muff was part Maine Coon cat and grew quite large yet he somehow could fit in the trivia box as we played the game that was all the rage.

In the seventeen years we shared, Muff grew to weigh seventeen pounds. When I took him wrapped in a blanket to the vet, people thought I was carrying a raccoon. Now a city girl, my cats ate high-grade cat food and had regular checkups. Once a year I asked the technician to bathe him. With the conditioner his fur turned silky. Muff good-naturedly endured the bow she placed around his neck. This ritual started to cure a case of fleas.

He had picked up the fleas when I'd left him at a cattery while I spent two weeks in Winnipeg. I was still naïve in the world of cats and hadn't thought to put a flea collar on him; he was after all an indoor cat. When I returned to collect him, Judy exclaimed, "He's been playing with the kittens all week."

As I stooped down to pet a little kitten, Muff bounded around a corner and knocked the kitten aside. He head butted me. I had not only been recognized; I had been claimed.

Never a lap cat, as Muff aged he grew more affectionate and cuddly. One day I arrived home to see David sprawled on the couch with Muff lying on his chest.

"Look what I taught him," David shouted.

Later Muff transferred this affectionate manner to me. I was lucky as animals relate differently to everyone; just as our relationships with people are all unique so are our animal-to-people relationships. Muff developed a special behavior with me. Every morning he would stand on my chest and lightly touch my cheeks with his paw to awaken me. He was more reliable and more fun than an alarm clock.

During a routine checkup, the vet diagnosed Muff with kidney disease and put him on a special diet. I wish she'd explained the consequences. I'd been under a lot of stress and had not noticed changes in his behavior. Cats are stalwart. Maybe it's instinctive not to show pain or loss of strength. The only way we can monitor their health is to note changes in diet, toilet habits and behavior, then get them into the vets. Ignorance does not assuage guilt.

I'd noticed he was sluggish, not climbing up the stairs to sleep at the foot of the bed. The night before I left on vacation, I thought it peculiar he drank so much water. His feet looked flat. He was dehydrating from the disease and needed an I.V. but I didn't see it. He was especially affectionate. Was he saying goodbye? Do animals know? He had crawled into my closet when the neighbors found him.

I had never experienced deep grief at the loss of anyone. I did for Muff. I cycled through all the stages: denial, anger, depression, bargaining, acceptance. I attended grief counseling and even located a self-help organization for people dealing with the loss of a pet. In our culture, people don't know how to treat a grieving person, but a person grieving the loss of a pet, no one understood. The pain took months to work through. I'd lost a best friend, a member of the family.

I knew I could not replace Muff but the house echoed. I wanted another cat. I visited the SPCA, the Humane Society. I looked into the yearning faces who wanted nothing more than a home. I spent time petting and trying to relate to all manner of cats but made no connections. Perhaps I wasn't ready emotionally? Perhaps it was time to search for my dream cat? I liked going to cat shows. I had often thought of getting a little sister for Muff but wondered if he could adjust. I remember my own sibling rivalry growing up. I had a card from a breeder upstairs somewhere in a drawer.

We made an appointment to see this breeder located a two-hour drive outside of Toronto. I quickly learned the etiquette. You don't select a kitten; the breeder approves you. Then there is the waiting list. We had to remove our shoes and wear slippers. As we toured the immaculate cattery, which was once a garage, I marvelled at the cages of white and silver Chinchilla Persians. Each cage had a name plate and the names were fanciful–Destiny, Duchess, Dolly. Joy was de-caged and I was allowed to hold her and given a lesson in grooming. Persians have two coats of fur and need daily combing. Then I was questioned and filled out suitable forms.

As we left the breeder remarked, "You're the only person who spoke to and petted each one of my cats."

I think I had passed approval without trying.

Two months later the phone call came.

"We have a kitten available; can you come this weekend?" the caller asked. Plans were changed so indeed we could. I felt like an adoptive mother.

Four little fluff balls romped in a large bottomless cage on the living room carpet. I was told that they were being "socialized." Among the three silvery white kittens was a tiny pure white one with huge saucer-shaped blue eyes. I waited in anticipation. The breeder lifted the tiny white kitten out.

"This little girl is pure Chin," the breeder said. "We were going to raise her as a breed cat but her tail developed a kink–she's pet quality."

To me she was perfect.

As we drove out of sight, I took her out of the carrier, placing her on my heart. Her tiny body was so warm. Perhaps it's what a mother feels when the doctor puts the newborn over her abdomen. All I know is that we bonded in that moment.

I'd been going to name her Kismet but it didn't fit. David suggested Guinevere–a fine lady, a queen. Strange how we shorten or give nicknames to those we love. Soon Guinevere was Gwenie. This was fitting as my father's favorite aunt was Aunt Gwenie and my high school English teacher and mentor was Gwen Rattle–both fine ladies.

Gwenie was everything you would want in a cat–gentle, sweet-tempered, playful, affectionate. She became my surrogate child, my companion, and my respite. When I returned from work exhausted, she'd greet me happily and lift my spirit. As she lay on my chest, her sweetness soothed my stress. I laughed out loud as she batted ping pong balls like hockey pucks. I smiled as she pranced, her paws in the air like a fine Arabian horse as she sat on the corner of my armchair.

She was a quiet animal and would sit for hours on my lap on the patio or laze on the grass under a tree. For the five brief years that she lived, she filled my life with love and joy. They say a parent shouldn't have to bury a child; it is the cruellest loss. I have never fully recovered from her passing. It was a frigid January day. It was the worst day of my life.

One spring day a huge orange cat sauntered up my driveway. I fed him. Soon he started appearing regularly for late lunches. He'd figured out my schedule. He seemed a stray but bore a collar with a phone number. His owners left him outside for hours in the worst kind of weather. To me, he was neglected, an emotional stray. I've always felt that owning a domestic animal is a commitment. Leo was the bridge until I was ready for another cat. I could love him just a little.

It can be difficult to find kittens at shelters; spring is the best time. I remember seeing a breed called Birman at a cat show. I was attracted to their long silky cream-colored fur and gentle temperament. Birmans are related to the ancient temple cats of Burma. They have color point markings like Siamese, but are loyal and highly sociable, referred to as "the Labradors of the cat world."

I wanted another white kitten but knew the folly in it. I needed a new cat and a new start. I went on the Internet to locate breeders and an upcoming cat show. As I spoke with one particular breeder at the show, I learned the qualities of the breed. I also made a connection with the breeder.

"Can you come up next Sunday?" he asked. "We usually don't show kittens at seven weeks but..."

It turned out he wanted to keep the kitten in question as it resembled the prize-winning show cat mother, but his wife wanted to sell her. Peculiar how the world of purebred cats works. He was willing to sell her to me.

Five cats greeted me. These breeders didn't believe in cages. Cats were everywhere–on perches, on couches, lazing on the cool hardwood floors of this immaculate house.

I saw her instantly. At twelve weeks, she was the tiniest of the two litters, all creamy white with a dollop of slate grey on her nose and the biggest and bluest eyes. The rest scuttled about as she hid timidly under the coffee table. We were a match.

When I drove her home, I wasn't so sure. She cried loudly to escape the carrier but wouldn't settle on my lap. It was an hour and a half of bedlam. Once home, Rebecca took a circular pass around the living room, jumped into my lap and began purring. She looked up with "It's okay; I'll stay" in her eyes.

She sits now, half on my feet and half on the comforter as I write. Rebecca is the most demanding of all the cats in my life. This playful imp tosses fluff balls around late at night, scoring soccer goals. She dashes from window to window chasing squirrels. She knocks over vases, drinks water from the dripping tap, chews curtains, cries for me to lift the blanket so she can curl up underneath and rattles her leash to go outdoors when the sun shines. She knows what she wants and has excellent communication skills. Her behaviors make me laugh. She makes me stop and notice.

When I arrive home, she promptly rolls over for a tummy rub. At night watching TV, she lays in my arms like a baby, placing her paw around my neck. I try not to pet her upon entry until I've washed my hands. After returning from a two-week vacation, I hit the bathroom first to wash my hands, and she jumps on the toilet, crying loudly as she stands on the toilet seat trying to reach me. As I take her in my arms, she purrs and licks my face. Now if that's not love, what is!

Someone gave me a fridge magnet that reads: "Cats are little people in fur coats."

Sometimes I prefer cats to people, for their love is pure and unconditional.

© 2011 Gail B. Murray. Used with permission of author. Gail Murray is a freelance writer based in Toronto. Her poems have been published in Canadian Authors Association Toronto branch's *Wordscape* and Canadian Poetry Society's *Arborealis*. Creative non-fiction and travel pieces have appeared in *The Globe and Mail*, *Trellis* and *NOW Magazine*.

# Cricket

I was thirteen-years old boy, about as sad as I had ever been. It was 1961 and my dad and stepmother had just moved the fall before to a large ranch-style home on Highway 2 in Pickering, just east of Toronto. They had bought me a pretty little dog named Sandy, who was of mixed breed but mostly cocker spaniel. One day I'd gone across the two-lane highway to talk to some kids on the other side and taken Sandy with me. After a few minutes I thought to check where she was and was horrified to see that she'd gone back to our place. In a panic I called her without looking, only to realize a car was bearing down on her. I called out to try to get her to stop, but it was too late. The guilt was horrible and the pain of the loss was too.

After a while Dad decided to get another dog to replace Sandy. A friend told him he wanted to find a new home for his cocker spaniel because she was having a hard time coping with his six rough-housing kids. It seems they'd play with her then stuff

291

her in the basement when they didn't want to look after her. I imagine the kids weren't being mean; they were young kids with no sense that a pup needed loving just like another kid. This is especially true of cocker spaniels as anyone who owns one probably knows; they are often smart, but highly strung, and are very affected by their surroundings.

Dad and I went over to his friend's place and sat down in the living room where I had my first introduction to Cricket.

The Botts had a bare hardwood floor in the hallway, polished to a house-proud shine and somewhat slippery. A small throw rug lay near the stairs to the basement. They called Cricket up and she came charging toward the living room like a hyperactive runaway missile, hit the throw rug just as she decided the appropriate way to greet everybody was to sit up. She slid past the door on the rug at a fair turn of speed, sitting up and tail wagging, ears flopping and tongue hanging out in frantic excitement. It was clear, even to a thirteen-year-old boy that she was over-stimulated, nervous, and although friendly, a train wreck just the same.

Despite any misgivings we had, we took her home. The same day we headed up to our cottage on Faraday Lake near Bancroft, a three and a half hour drive, with a shivering excited dog in the back with me. I remember looking at her and I guess I wondered if she could ever replace Sandy in my heart. Cricket was all golden with big brown eyes (when she'd hold still long enough so you could look into them) and I had to admit she was really beautiful. My stepmom was pretty sceptical and she insisted that we'd see how the weekend went but that she was leaning toward returning Cricket on Monday. That didn't feel great to me, but I knew I wouldn't get a vote if she was against the dog. I guess I couldn't really blame her either with Cricket's hyperactivity and nervousness. However, after stopping en route for dinner, we made it to the cottage and carried everything in. I kept an eye on Cricket; actually I'm pretty sure I had her on a leash for fear this city dog would take off and promptly get lost in the forest surrounding our cottage.

I can't remember whether it was spring or fall but it was one or the other because it was cold out, especially at night. This was back in the days when people had coal stoves in cottage country; we'd buy bags of coal in nearby Bancroft, a uranium mining town where one section of the sidewalk was wooden slats like in the old west. We bought ice for our fridge (not ice cubes, but a great big block of ice to stick in what would now be the freezer in a modern fridge) and that would keep the fridge cold and the food edible for the weekend. There was no electric fridge in cottage country unless you trucked in earth and put a lawn around your cottage so delivery trucks could get in. We were purists with nothing but trees around and we had regular deliveries of the ice when we were up for the summer. There were electric lights and a propane stove for cooking, so you had to know how to light it properly with a match or you'd be in orbit with your shirt and eyebrows on fire.

Coal stoves may not be considered a good idea now but I loved them and that's what we had to keep us warm. Stoves weren't as efficient as they are now but it didn't matter. Once you got your coal stove going you only had to stoke it once in the morning and once in the evening, and the chimney would glow red hot and you'd be as warm as toast. We had thick blankets for early morning when it would get freezing as the fire burned low.

We all went to bed. Dad had stoked the stove up for the night and each of us went to our own bedroom with Cricket being left to find whatever spot she wanted to settle in. By morning I was huddled under the blankets to stay warm in the frigid cottage and waiting for Dad to do his magic. You see our tradition was that Dad got up first and stoked the stove and then often went back to bed or down to the lake to get water for breakfast while the cottage heated up enough for us to get up and dressed quickly (very quickly). But this morning was different.

Dad got up all right but realized after he'd done with the stove that he couldn't find Cricket and started quietly looking for her while trying not to wake my stepmom. He poked his head into her room and started to snort and laugh, I'd been following all this because there were no real walls in the cottage, just dividers and although I couldn't make out what they were saying I got the sense that something was up. I jumped out of bed, put on my slippers and went to her room to see my Dad moving aside to let me in while still laughing. Right beside my stepmom on the pillow and under the blankets was Cricket, blissfully warm and sound asleep. Seems she had been fine for a while until very early in the morning when the cold got too much, and the next thing my stepmom heard was her door being nosed hesitantly aside, and then Cricket's head and paws peeked over the edge of the bed while she shivered so hard she was almost the first dog to have her teeth chatter. She then laid her head on the pillow beside my bemused stepmom and gazed into her face with those big liquid brown eyes you could get lost in. My stepmom noticed a scratching sound and when she looked down, she caught a hind paw trying to get purchase on the bed. Cricket was taking nothing for granted, I think she knew she could be turned down and that meant staying cold; so she had a lot at stake and was hesitant. One thing led to another, and within a few seconds my stepmom found herself opening the blankets for a freezing, shivering little dog and Cricket dived in probably thinking she was in dog heaven.

In case you were wondering, there was no question of Cricket going back to the Botts. When my Father jokingly reminded my stepmom of this possibility, she got a gleam in her eye that made it clear it would be a lot more likely my dad would be going there rather than Cricket if he pushed things. Not a chance, because Dad had also fallen for our little blonde lady (as she fell for him over the next while), and I, of course, knew I had a special girl to replace Sandy. I had no idea how much.

# Cricket and Her Kids

In the course of time, our dog Cricket came into heat. I don't know about my parents, but at thirteen years old I wasn't a veteran dog owner. I didn't know how to be a chaperone for a good-looking golden blonde who caused amorous male dogs to magically emerge out of the woods around our cottage. At first it seemed weird how they all appeared to know about her availability, but it gradually became a bit annoying. However, it turned into much more when I caught her in the parking lot where she was hooked to a male who took off in panic, dragging her after him and screaming in pain while he ran.

After that we found out she was pregnant. We became excited and set about adapting to an expansion of the family. Our girl was having pups! I'm sure she was the calmest of us all. Dad set about making a nest for her in our rec room where she could have them. One day soon after, she wanted to come downstairs with me when I went there to watch TV. I remember holding onto her short tail as she waddled down the steep stairs; by then she was so big I didn't know if she could make it by herself without tumbling. I wanted her to get used to the hospital pen (and I guess practice being ready myself), so I lifted her over the one-foot-high chicken fence surrounding the large cardboard box on its side and placed her inside among all the torn-up newspaper that would serve as a bed. It really was a great hospital bed Dad had made and she seemed right at home. I started to watch television, and after a while decided to go over and see how she was in her new mansion. To my shock and excitement I saw a little blind, bare fellow crawling up from between her legs toward her belly, and she was calmly licking it clean. I thundered upstairs to let anyone home know the she was bringing the puppies into the world and then charged back down wild with excitement for her and to watch our very own science show.

There were five pups altogether: two nondescript-looking black ones with a bit of white and three gorgeously coloured black, white and brown ones. There were three males and two females. This began the adventures of the whole family as we kept two of the pups, one of the multi-coloured males, Charlie, and one of the plain blacks, Suzy.

Charlie, as I said, was beautiful, even his head was black, white and brown. He had magnificent black eyebrows and a proud white flag of a tail. He was all heart, courageous, affectionate and friendly to everyone, but God made up for his over-abundance of gifts by making him dumb as a post. He was like a big affectionate over-muscled youngster who would love to go everywhere with you but couldn't spell his own name. His heart and handsomeness made anyone forget about that. His loyalty to his family, which included us, and his loving, fearless nature made him dear to everybody.

Suzy though, hmm, well never was there such a lesson in the folly of underestimating someone because of looks. She was plain black with just a white blaze on her chest and Dad, for some reason I never understood, had her tail cropped like Cricket's and like most Cocker Spaniels are, I guess. She made up for her lack of looks though, by carrying the wickedest tricky intelligence between her ears I've ever seen in an animal, or most humans for that matter. She clearly took after Cricket in smarts, but turned to a mischief her mom never felt the need for.

I can give you some examples. If Suzy had been locked in one of those German prisoner of war camps in World War Two she'd have driven her captors crazy because she was a one-dog escape committee. She naturally figured pens and fences were put there for her amusement and recreation, so gaily set about frustrating any efforts to keep her in. The first time I became aware of this was shortly after the pups' birth. Nearly every day we let them out of the pen they'd been born in so they could explore around our big ranch-style house. When they'd been cuddled and made a fuss over we would herd them back to their home downstairs in the pen. Cricket could jump over the low fence around it to feed and care for them, then jump out when she wanted a break. That was when I noticed something off. After I had put all the pups in the pen there always seemed to be one little black one I'd forgotten. I gradually smelled a rat and decided to set a trap. I placed them all in the big pen and walked across the room to the door, ducked down behind the big stone bar right beside it, and opened and closed the door to imitate going out. Then I quickly scurried across to the other end of the bar and peeked over. The pups were all scrambling over each other about their business except one fat little black one, Suzy. She sat there intently staring at where I had disappeared. Then she reared up on her hind legs and grabbed as high up on the chicken wire as she could with her claws, and to my amazement, started to pull herself up the fence. She reached the board that ran along the top, grasped it with her paws and pulled herself up onto it. She teetered there, rocking back and forth while balancing on her chubby tummy. Then she gave a kick and toppled over the board and fell out, landing in a sprawl, spread out on the floor outside of the pen. She excitedly picked herself up and high-tailed it for the door, although where she thought she was going through a closed door I don't know. I quickly moved to the door, and as she frantically scrabbled around the corner I levelled my finger at her and in my strictest early teenager voice said, "Suzy!" She slammed her bum down on the floor and skidded to a halt. Busted. As she slid along, she curled her lip and frantically grinned at me while wagging her whole back end as she coasted to a stop. This became her signature trick whenever she was caught at something or was just embarrassed. She would curl her upper lip and grin as if to say "Who me?" Over the next few years we saw this performance many times.

That was the beginning of trying to keep her confined. When the pups were old enough to go outside, Dad built a pen around the back door enclosing the concrete pad leading from the door to the garage. The pen extended out into the grass for a couple of meters or so and thus made a space perhaps 4 by 3 meters. He covered it in sand so they could use it as an outdoor toilet. The sand made it easy to clean as it dried out the results and they could be scooped with a grass rake onto a shovel. Guess whose job that was.

Anyhow, he'd made the fence about 2½ metres high, to frustrate Suzy mainly, and figured he had her beat, but only days after the pups started using it we saw her rambling around the backyard and looking madly curious while Charlie barked at her because he wanted to come too. We let them out again later and looked to see what was happening and saw that Suzy would get her mother and Charlie playing and running after her and then she'd lead them in a charge against the fence. The fence heeled over and before it could come back up Suzie continued right up and over it to freedom.

Charlie looked around frantically wondering where she'd vanished to while Cricket just sat down calmly to watch her wonder kid go for an exploration of the big back yard!

Dad reinforced the fence but she just climbed over it. Next he put some more chicken wire along the top and angled it back into the pen so she couldn't possibly get out. That stopped her for a day or two and then there she was trotting around the backyard with what I'd swear was a smirk on her face.

Again I laid a trap by peeking around the side of the house just in time to see her run at the brick wall where the pen joined the brick, jump as high as she could and ricochet off the bricks over the fence. Dad grumbled and chuckled in admiration and piled all the garden tools in that spot to foil her again. A day or so later we found a huge hole bigger than her dug beside the fence. However, this time Dad had her beat because when he'd first put the pen in he'd dug a trench to set the wire in and it was too deep for her to dig under. Finally vanquished, Suzie cheerfully begged me to take them for walks so she could get out on parole.

Our house was on Highway 2 in Pickering, Ontario and behind us lay nothing but fields so I could easily take the dogs on a walk of several kilometers if I wanted to. On one of the first of these hikes with the still chubby pups and Cricket, as we crossed a quiet street, a fairly big dog came charging out from one of the houses and attacked Suzy. Charlie dropped whatever he was doing and piled in to help his sister and I saw that both of them were getting whipped by this bigger adult dog. I was a little alarmed that my beloved family would get hurt, so began running to the rescue. Then I suddenly remembered to look for Cricket. To my surprise she was sitting on the other side of the street and calmly observing how her pups were doing. It occurred to me that if she wasn't worried, why should I be? I stopped to see how she handled this situation. After a few moments she stood up and started to quietly walk toward the fur ball of three dogs fighting. Then she broke into a trot, and by the time she reached them she had hit full charge and bowled the other dog over. Then it was team time as Cricket took on the bigger dog face to face. Charlie was draped over its back industriously (and probably uselessly) gnawing on its backbone. Suzy was fastened on to the dog's tail with her sharp little baby teeth and hung on for dear life as it whipped her around

305

through the air. I could hear the enemy dog howling through its growls at the pain Suzy's little needle teeth must have been causing it. Finally, it saw the light and gave up, shook off the family and ran full tilt for home and safety. Cricket then gathered the kids up and we set off to complete our walk, victors over the field, and with me so proud I could bust.

# Heloise, the Guide Dog Puppy

Hi. I'm Heloise, a yellow lab puppy born at Guide Dogs for the Blind in California. When I was just three weeks old, some very friendly and specially-trained people began cuddling me and whispering sweet nothings into my ears. Bet you didn't know puppies learn more quickly and bond with humans better when we are handled gently while very young, did you? This type of interaction with humans actually makes more synapses in our brains. And, as you know, we guide dogs have to be extremely smart, and this is one of the tricks of the trade.

At about five weeks I went on short walks exploring our campus, but I must say I wasn't a pro on the leash then. My handlers were gentle and patient while I bounded about smelling the flowers and bushes.

At eight weeks I went on a long ride with my siblings and friends all the way to Colorado. If you ever see our puppy truck,

307

you will recognize it right away because it is big, holds eighteen puppies, and has *my* baby picture on it! The puppy truck really *is* very special. Not just because of my photo, but also because the puppies inside will forever change people's lives. When we arrived in Colorado, I saw smiles, tears and cameras everywhere. Everyone was so emotional! Well, I must say, after those three days on the truck, I was, too. I kissed my new puppy-raising Mom again and again before I became so exhausted from all the excitement that I fell asleep in her arms.

Puppy raisers are often goofy at the puppy truck. Some raisers have reared many puppies, so this is D-Day (Dreaded Day) when they have to trade their grown-up puppy for a replacement puppy. Some people are receiving their first puppy to raise and are nervous. Emotions run high! When we came off the truck one by one, we heard enough "Oohs" and "Ahs" to make you think you were at the Miss America contest.

What fun I had when we got home! A huge yard to play in with grass where I could "do my business," flowers to sniff, and even another dog to play with! My older sister is named Aspen, and she has helped Mom raise about ten other puppies before me, and I might add here that she is pretty strict. No chewing on her ears thank you! In the backyard, Mom told me, "Do your business," and when I did it on the grass, you'd have thought I had won the Boston Marathon! She was ecstatic! Humans are strange. My Lab mom didn't care where I did my business; but this was some kind of big deal I could tell, so I worked hard to always please Mom.

The next year went by in a whirl! I've been just about everywhere starting with church. In the beginning I had to sit with Mom in the cry room, but guess what? I was a baby myself, so I had fun licking the other babies' faces and making them laugh. Soon I sat out with everyone else, but I had to be a "good girl," which meant no chewing, playing, or barking. Naptime! Nothing against the minister, I heard he is good.

During the next year, I went to lots of puppy meetings where I saw my friends and learned all sorts of neat stuff. For example, at the outside mall, I learned not to bark at the skateboarders, bicyclers or the fire truck, and, how to walk over those scary grates, walk up open stairs (yikes). But the hardest part for me was learning not to snag the ice cream cones the little kids were holding. I admit that I did try a couple of times; but Mom was quick. Bummer. No ice cream for me. But, they smelled so good!

The inside malls had all sorts of interesting stuff like toys that talked, funny people that did not smell like people (I heard someone call them statues), floors that changed colors, and see-through elevators. Sometimes I was scared, but Mom was patient and always showed me I was safe; and I really trust my mom.

Mom retired from an airline and has friends everywhere, so wow, I became a good traveler. I went to a Polish wedding in Chicago (I do not polka, thank you); Yosemite where I met lots of nice tourists who asked to pet me, and, when I was a perfect lady, I did get petted; Las Vegas (pretty lights but very crowded); New York City (boy, was *that* an experience!). I am now a pro when it comes to airports, buses, planes, trains, automobiles, and subways.

I visited many places close to home, too. Every day was filled with new experiences that we practiced until I was a pro. We visited the doctor's office, the grocery store where, I must say, I'm *so* good at staying by those onions while Mom gets the tomatoes. I also went to concerts, banks, and restaurants, with restaurants being the most challenging because, despite all the great-smelling things that were on the table, I had to just lie on the floor and act disinterested. Not fun at all if you ask me! Mom tells me I am the best puppy she has raised, but I bet she says that to all of them.

Of course I wasn't always a perfect puppy I must admit. One time, on a trip to visit Mom's friend, I thought I was being so sneaky and wouldn't get caught. Here is the scene: Mom and Dad were sleeping, and my rule is to always have "four on the floor," but one morning I snuck onto the top of the bed, behind the pillows, so slowly (this took about twenty minutes…..hard work it was) I thought they wouldn't notice. I was laid out across the top of the bed and I was so proud of myself……but then, they opened their eyes, and started laughing so hard at me and then pointed to the ground. Bam! I had been caught as they had been watching me the whole time. Bah humbug!

One day we went for a ride, and I saw the puppy truck again. You remember that truck, right? The one with my picture on it? Mom whispered tearfully in my ear, "See you at graduation." I didn't understand why she was crying and hugging me so. That day I left on a three-day ride which took me back to the school where I was born.

My goodness, I was a busy girl for the next six months. I had to learn about curbs, stairs, cars, sidewalks, obstacles on the street AND above my person's head. I learned about how to guide a person at night, in the rain, in the mall, and on country roads with no sidewalks at all. I also had to learn the most important lesson of all which is TO DISOBEY A COMMAND IF MY PERSON MADE A MISTAKE. This is called "Intelligent Disobedience" and it is what distinguishes us guide dogs from all the rest of the dogs in the world. My final exam took place in San Francisco amidst the noisy cable cars and all the distractions. The tests were hard but I passed!

After all my hard work I was assigned to *my very own* person. She's different from my puppy-raising mom, but she loves me; that I can tell. Her name is Pat. She hugs me and praises me a lot. We worked together for a month before the big day... Graduation! Can I tell you a little about it?

What an occasion it was! Over one hundred people were there, and we dogs were the center of attention, up on the stage beside our visually impaired people. Everybody gave a speech (well, not us dogs, of course). There wasn't a dry eye in the house. First, the recipients thanked everybody for their dog (tears), then each puppy raiser made a speech about how happy they were that their "baby" made it (more tears), and finally, we (the dogs) gave a demonstration about how guide dogs actually work. Everybody was so happy! There was a lot of crying and hugging going around. You get the picture, right? Lots of Kleenex. Kleenex on every flat surface actually. Humans are weird. None of us dogs cried.

Now I am official, harness and all. I look nothing like the little puppy I was when I left California about eighteen months ago. I have been a busy girl with so much to learn, but it was all worth it because now I have a wonderful life serving as my friend Pat's eyes. I love Pat lots. I get to go everywhere with her, which makes me one happy dog.

Now that you know my story, I'd like to say thanks for listening, and hey, would you do me a favor? Honk and wave if you see the puppy truck on the road between California and Denver.

Love, Heloise

(Transcribed by puppy raiser "Mom," Jill Nieglos)

# Heloise

Hi. I am Heloise, all grown up and working as Pat's guide dog, since she was forty-eight. At the age of two, she had cancer and lost both of her eyes, so my job is imperative to Pat. I have heard that some people don't really understand what a guide dog does, so I would like to share some stories of my daily life.

You need to know that guide dogs and their special people have a bond that is indescribable as we depend on one another to live our lives. I serve as Pat's eyes, but I bet you thought I know when the light turns green. Ha! Fooled you! I don't. I have been trained for "Intelligent Disobedience," which means that if Pat makes a mistake when we are on the road, I am in charge, but of safety, not how to get from place to place.

Here is the real scoop: when we are close to a curb I pause just momentarily. Through the strong harness I wear, Pat can tell when I do pause, so she stops and puts her foot out to see what's up or down, as the case may be.

*Ah, it's a down curb. Got it*, she thinks. So she stops and waits for the traffic sounds crossing in front of her to cease, then waits a couple more seconds, and says, "Forward."

Because I have great eyes and am strong too, both qualifications of a guide dog, I look both ways to determine if she has made a good decision before we enter the street. I decide "Yes," so we start to cross the street. This works 99.9 per cent of the time. However, every now and then a crisis occurs.

One time that exact scenario happened after we started crossing the street. A car turned right on the red light. We were in the middle of the street, but I saw it and shoved Pat about twelve feet back out of the street. Sorry to say she landed on her behind; however, neither of us was injured, thankfully, and I got a steak for dinner! I have actually done that three times for Pat in my very long career of twelve years. Usually a guide dog's career is about eight years, so I received bonus time of four years.

On another occasion something very odd happened, and I rescued her in a different way. We went for a taxi ride one night and I sat in my usual spot on the floor behind the passenger seat right in front of

Pat. Pat had asked the driver to take her to Suzy's house which was only about ten minutes away, but the ride seemed longer. Although we were in a city, Pat noticed there was no more traffic noise outside. I could tell she was getting nervous. Then the driver turned off the engine. Dead silence. I could tell that Pat was scared.

"Where are we?" she asked the driver in an agitated voice.

He didn't answer. No sound came from the front seat. Now I knew something was wrong, and I wasn't going to let anybody hurt my Pat. I jumped on her lap, hackles up, protecting her with my sixty-five pounds.

"Where are we? Where are we?" she kept asking the man.

No answer! For the first time in my life I growled at a person and I showed him every tooth I had. Pat called 911 on her cell, and they immediately traced the call. The man started the engine and took us to our destination. We later heard he was fired the next day. My Pat was safe! I was proud.

I can cop an attitude every now and then because I know I am good. One time we were in Minneapolis and had to visit an office located in a tall set of twin towers. Pat thought she knew where she was going, but remember, I am the one with the eyes, and I knew we were in the wrong building. So I hesitated to go where she commanded. However, I obeyed her because I knew she was safe. We went up to 2401, entered and she asked for Mr. Zacket.

"Ah, you are in the wrong tower," the receptionist said. "Mr. Zacket is in the other tower."

Harrumph. I took Pat out of that office in one big hurry, down the elevator and straight to the other tower. I walked very fast because I KNEW where we were going. She huffed and puffed but we arrived there on time. She did apologize to me later, though.

Well, I did tell you I have an attitude, right? Yes, I did; I remember.

Another time we went to the doctor's office. Pat always sat in a particular chair, but this time some lady was already sitting there. I just stood and stared at that lady, like *Why on earth would you be sitting in my Pat's chair?*

"Oh my goodness," she said. "Your dog seems to think she wants you to sit in this chair."

"No, it isn't a big deal," Pat said. "I usually do sit there. However, you just sit there. She will get used to it."

I just kept staring at that lady who had the audacity to sit in *my* Pat's chair until she finally decided to move to another chair.

I love babies. No, I LOVE babies, and I worry about them. If I hear one crying and Pat is going somewhere, well, we first have to see if the baby is all right. Shopping in Costco sometimes gets a bit tiresome for Pat, as I just HAVE to check on all the babies. After all, I started out my "professional" career pacifying all the babies in the cry room of the church.

I have another idiosyncrasy. I get a cookie every night at 7 p.m. I am never a minute early or a minute late. I know when 7 p.m. is and every evening I wait for my treat exactly on time in front of the cookie jar. But twice a year people seem to forget when 7 p.m. is. I heard them say something about daylight savings time but it certainly annoys me to have to change my schedule. I guess dogs just don't understand time changes.

I also have a perfect memory.

One time Pat said to me, "Let's go to Arlene's house."

Her house was about seven or eight blocks away. We hadn't stopped there for a year or more, but I led her perfectly up three blocks, left four blocks, then to the third house on the right and up the steps. She couldn't believe it when we arrived at Arlene's house in about ten minutes. Sometimes I amaze myself and I always amaze Pat.

I must admit that I am not always so perfect. There was that time at my third birthday party when they went outside to hang the balloons so guests could see we were the birthday house. While they were gone, well, I helped myself to about one third of my cake. I ask you, whose birthday cake was it anyway? I don't know why everybody made such a fuss about that cake having big bites out of it. Boy, carrot cake with vanilla frosting is delicious, but the candles were a little crunchy.

Near my twelfth birthday I started feeling not so great. Pat called my puppy raiser mom and dad to visit me. I had seen them about once a year and Pat and I had stayed with them three times in Colorado, so I was very happy to see them, and I really enjoyed the duck treats they brought me too. After their visit I began feeling just a teeny bit worse every day, and within two months I didn't feel well at all. Then the worst thing of all happened. Pat went away and left me with some other people.

Where was my Pat?

She departed on a Monday and hadn't returned home on Friday, so I gave up and refused to eat or drink. I felt there was no reason to live without my beloved Pat. I didn't know it but she was very sick and in the hospital. These other people called the vet as I couldn't walk anymore. The vet suggested that they take me to the hospital to see my beloved Pat. They wheeled me into her room in a wheelchair, and I had the most wonderful surprise. There, in a funny white bed lay my Pat. They lifted me up onto the bed with her and I kissed her over and over and wiggled for a long time. I was very happy and content, and so was Pat. When my visiting time with Pat was over, these other people took me back to the vet's office because I was quite ill. Many people petted me and told me what a good dog I was, but I felt so tired, and I finally went to sleep for the last time.

I know Pat still misses me because she talks to me every day and I always listen quietly and send her good thoughts.

Heloise, the guide dog of Pat.

Jill Nieglos

# Lilo, the Guide Dog Puppy with the Sixth Sense

I am a woman who raises guide dog puppies for the blind, and a puppy-in-training is allowed to go anywhere a guide dog can go, so when I got the call that my mother had had a stroke and was in the hospital in Dallas, "Lilo" (the only puppy I had raised who had not met my mom) and I left quickly for the plane trip to Dallas.

When I entered the hospital with my dad, I received the normal reaction I always get when people see a puppy-in-training: smiles from everyone. The doctors, nurses, receptionist, and orderlies all smiled, no they grinned at us, and, everyone came running to pet the puppy. While doing this volunteer work, I have noticed that it always seems to lighten people's hearts to see a beautiful and well-behaved puppy in the training process.

On this night though, we needed to hurry, so we were quickly ushered upstairs to Mom's room. She lay in a bed covered with a mesh canopy, which was secured for her own protection. Mom was startled when we entered the room and fell to the edge of the mesh. There was another patient in the room, but Lilo went directly to my mom and started licking her arm through the mesh. Lilo usually does not lick, so this was a curious response.

The nurse undid the canopy so we could hold Mom's hand. When she did, Lilo put her paws up on the side of the bed and systematically licked her entire arm. My mom did not recognize me at that moment, but she put her arms around the dog and tried to speak. We guess she was saying, "puppy, puppy, puppy," but just "pha" sounds came out, as she had lost speech with her stroke. I was touched but quite bewildered. How could Lilo possibly have known which person was my mother? She did not even look in the direction of the other person in the room before making a beeline for my mother.

After this very thorough greeting, Lilo decided even a more close-up approach was needed. I was surprised because after all the training I had given her for the last year (the rule is always to have four feet on the floor), she tried to get up on the bed with

Mom. I stopped her three times, when the nurse turned to me.

"Oh, goodness," she said. "That would be the best thing for your mom, so do please let her get up."

Up she went. That is when she really did her best work. She lay down next to Mom with her belly facing up and snuggled her neck up to my mom's neck. We fixed Mom's arm so she had it around the puppy, and for the next thirty minutes or so, our little world was perfect. Peace and love surrounded all of us while I showed Mom some important family pictures of Dad and her with my kids, which I had grabbed while trying to hurry out of the house to get to the airport. I thought this was a good alternative to conversation, as she had lost her speaking ability with the stroke. Mom was happy. Dog was happy. Dad was happy. I was happy. The nurse had tears in her eyes.

Finally the time came to say our goodbyes. The nurse had to put the mesh canopy back up, so we waved to Mom through the mesh and told her we would see her the next morning. This was when Lilo decided one more kiss was imperative, and pulled against the leash. I let her go. Again she went back to Mom's bed, put her paws up on the side of the bed and kissed her one more time up and down her arm through the mesh. I heard Mom sort of giggle.

That was the last time I saw my mother alive. The hospital called early the next morning to tell us she had had a massive stroke and passed away. I take great comfort in the fact that some of her last moments were spent with Dad and me, and especially with such a compassionate puppy, who somehow knew what my dying mother needed most: unconditional love.

Jill Nieglos

# Love between Species

At the beginning of my studies in primatology, even though I was a woman, I had the same attitudes and feelings about animals as everyone else. Cute, perhaps cuddly, to be taken care of, but certainly "other," and indeed "lesser" than human. I anticipated a career with laboratory subjects and keeping my observation detached. So I began my first lab research–dissecting hands of monkeys and apes to help me understand something about the evolution of the hand. Oddly, the more I dissected, the more *sacred* this organ seemed to become, until I could no longer cut into the dead, perfused remnant.

Perhaps this happened because I became increasingly aware of the cerebral connection between hand and mind. I first met monkeys in cages, and thought that environment "normal" for them, although I worked in Kenya, where monkeys roam wild. I also conducted experiments on caged animals, at a primate center in Covington, Louisiana. I wanted to know if monkeys were also mostly right-handed, as we are, which meant left-brained.

I used grain to see which hand they would reach with and presumed that would imply dominance. Monkeys are animals that browse all day long, and in this center they were fed enough to live, but not to fill up, and so they grabbed my experimental food with trembling hands. I had to give up the experiment and just feed them. I even conducted an experiment in my own lab, testing whether female monkeys were capable of orgasm. They are. This shared physiology underscored my closeness to them. Here was a basic biological function that was deeply ingrained in our primate history. Academia has rules, however, and going up against them incurs penalties. The reaction to this basic study left me reeling. I could not believe what was being said about me and my research, but I knew I had to change direction. I decided to leave the lab to study monkeys where they live–a safer intellectual environment, or so I thought.

When I was a child, my father used to regale my sister and me with stories of his travels and adventures. He had journeyed to the southern tip of Europe and seen monkeys there. It seemed a good place to start.

Now I was no longer an observer; I had become immersed in monkey life, subject to their rules and regulations, sensitive to their wants and even thoughts.

My first experience like this was with Mark, a macaque monkey in Gibraltar. This tiny point of land at the juncture of the Mediterranean and the Atlantic, the southernmost tip of Europe, was once crucial to the British Empire as a military outpost. The monkeys are nearly sacred because 300 years ago they played a role in protecting the empire, giving the alarm one night as the Spanish came to invade. "As the monkeys go, so goes the empire" was taken seriously, so when their numbers declined during World War II, Winston Churchill sent urgent messages demanding that more monkeys from their Moroccan homeland be brought over.

Mark was no youngster by the time I met him. He had been male leader of his matriarchy for a number of years. A formidable creature, he was bulky but nearly toothless; however, still strong enough to flip over a concrete boulder with a flick of his wrist, while I could barely move it. His fingers were gnarled, his gait lopsided; he obviously hurt when he walked but he had the energy to play with the "teenagers"–that bunch of adolescent males restive and eager to become full adults. His overhanging brow gave *gravitas* to his appearance, and a mere look from him was enough to send the toddlers running back to mum. On the other hand, he was as gentle as they come. It was his right to take babies away from their mothers on even the first day of life. I wasn't the first to note this male-care behavior, but was the first to see the significance in terms of group process. I knew the pattern existed in their relatives, the Moroccan monkeys, but also knew that they handled babies differently. The Gibraltar pattern was an extension of what I called "tradition drift," the further development of a local tradition. The theory acknowledges that behavior patterns are learned from generation to generation, and that individuals contribute to them by innovation. Mark's exercise of it developed it further, and established a pattern other males would see as youngsters and enact as adults. I found this exciting. It suggested that primatology theory was too narrow; too genetically based, and too dependent on undefined "instinct."

Mark carried the baby gingerly, holding it in a macho manner with one arm as he proceeded on three. He sat with the infant in his lap and made faces at the baby. These gestures were a prelude to learning group ways. His facial movement was inborn but his gestures and their meaning were taught. I began to understand the complexity of monkey life. He was totally at peace at these moments, his body relaxed and with what certainly must have been a smile on his old face. The mother hovered nearby, knowing her rights to take back the little one should it cry for comfort or more likely, milk. Reluctantly, Mark returned the baby, sitting beside the mother and grooming her, nattering again and again into the face of the little one.

Some days Mark sat beside me. His fur smelled of olives and his hands grasped my thigh. I did not budge. I knew the slightest movement might make him aware that he was touching, and I cherished the contact, the honor I felt had been bestowed on me breaching the distance. On the other hand, friend he might be, but a monkey nonetheless—an *other*. It was wise not to forget.

Some weeks earlier, a male student of mine had forgotten; had moved between a baby and its mother and gotten bitten in the thigh for his misbehavior. The few teeth that Mark still had included dagger-like canines. One day I did forget. I forgot *who* I was; that I was not them, but an intruder obliged to remember their rules, their codes. I moved too quickly. Someone, probably an impatient teen, eager to be responsible to the group, gave a warning bark and came at me. Mark moved quickly in front of him and rushed me. I did not think it possible for an elder to move so quickly. He grabbed my legs, looking straight into my eyes, his mouth slightly open, threatening.

"Don't Mark; please don't!" I cried.

And he let me go.

I ran away. Mark kept the group from following. My heart was in my mouth, and beating hard. He had kept me from real harm while fulfilling his role. It took some anxious days, but eventually I dared to return. I was forgiven, allowed back into their domain to sit and watch the babies grow, the politics of the females, the maneuverings of the young males.

Mark aged. One day he threatened the director of the nearby prison, and was judged "rogue."A sniper was sent out. Mark knew nothing as the bullet flew into his brain. Being woman, I was not allowed to watch, not even told this was about to occur. However, in **some incredible** involution, I was given the bullet casing that destroyed my friend, and most assuredly that is what he was—my *friend*. They had broken that bond–that single shot had ended Mark's life and our special relationship. I couldn't show any emotion because it wasn't "meet" to react to what was formal policy, but alone, I wept—for my friend and for our friendship. Somehow, the eons separating us, the cerebral structures, the very shape of our bodies were as nothing. We ate biscuits together, watched infants at play, juveniles clambering, sub-adults fighting, and felt the breeze, the cold of the Levant and the warmth of the sun. Isn't the basis of friendship sharing elemental things?

Some years later I received an answer. My father had traveled in the East, and so I knew monkeys roamed the parks of Kowloon, part of the territory and across the water from Hong Kong Island. As I left the airport a wall of steamy heat hit me; yet at times I shivered and wore socks for gloves because I did not know it could get that cold. The forest held nearly 600 monkeys. They had a complex history and genetic heritage. Anthropologists are used to obtaining information from arcane sources. I searched diaries, letters, newspapers, and of course, technical articles to detail their history. It turned out that these monkeys were the mixed offspring of several kinds of macaque monkeys that had been released in the name of Buddha, or were survivors protected by the fungshui forests during World War II. The colonial university did not take kindly to my insistence that they actually were hybrid monkeys; miscegenation just could not happen. In addition, I maintained that the monkeys lived in a large group, fragments of which were observable on any given day. The model I used here was that of an amoeba, whose leg-like pods flow into and out of the core body. The pods were these group fragments, and the observer could easily mistake a "pod" for an entire group. Academia can be a very cruel place and my notion was laughed at for being outrageous, ludicrous heresy! My students were upset; they *saw* what I described, and could not believe the reception my idea received. I took comfort in knowing that science has always been preceeded by its heretics.

For the monkeys, living amongst people guaranteed food, but also conflict. The certainty of being fed enabled the population to grow exponentially, and as it grew, the monkeys became more competitive for the handouts people brought or the picnics they carried and wanted to protect. People defended themselves with picnic forks or other objects.

One of the monkeys who got injured we called "Stump-arm."One of his limbs had been amputated by a machete; we did not know the circumstances; we only saw the result. He could negotiate on three limbs, but the wound still hurt. We suggested to the local authorities that perhaps they could capture him and repair the damage, which they were unwilling to do because it would cause far too much disruption in the group, and people coming to give gifts of oranges and other fruits to the monkeys would be alarmed.

But this narrative is not about human cruelty to animals; rather, it is about how the large, "bear" macaque female we called Phatty looked after him; how her caring and concern signified a friendship humans think impossible in other creatures.

Phatty and Stump-arm had been together for at least a decade by the time we watched them. He had a drawn face and was deeply fatigued. The wound, though not new, remained a fraction too long, bumped the ground as he walked or the trees as he climbed, clearly causing him pain. I winced in empathy, but there was nothing I could do. I wanted to hold him, to clean the wound, to give him painkillers. But if I tried to approach him, to do something to make him better, he would be frightened, then aggressive in self-defense. Phatty, however, could groom him. She operated gently and slowly, with a technique, it seemed, intended not to move him quickly which would cause more pain. She worked around the wound, cleaning, healing. They sat together for long moments, content in each other's company, secure that therein there was no tension. Together they surveyed the group. Stump-arm seemed to be revered by the young ones. They gathered near him; he chattered to them, and they would play at his feet. Mothers going off to feed left youngsters with this benign baby-sitter. He was a minor player in the game of status, but in terms of prestige, he clearly excelled. As for Phatty, perhaps her size alone clarified her role; perhaps something about her demeanor did the trick, but no one ever challenged her—a fact her daughter abused by tormenting others only to run and hide behind her formidable mother. Phatty always seemed to know where Stump-arm was and would gravitate towards him, to sit beside him, groom, and often hug. The odd thing was that in these hugs, Stump-arm, as often as not, was the one to do the patting on the back. The effort seemed to underscore the warmth and familiarity of their relationship. It was this bond, this taking the other for granted, this knowing the other was there, this support and caring, never worrying about mood or temper that defined their friendship.

The third part of this portrayal of love is also from Kowloon. Popeye was named before his eponymous tragedy. He was a young, newly matured male, part bear macaque, part long-tail and part rhesus as far as we could make out without a DNA test. Phatty may well have been his mother or at least his aunt as originally there had been two related adult female bear macaques. Popeye and Phatty spent a lot of time together, and he was very protective of her babies. My students and I never could get enough of observing him. There was something undeniably "good" about him— however, that may translate across species. He frequently played with the children, baby-sat when their mothers went off to feed, broke up fights between the young ones, and still had the time and inclination to climb trees, roughhouse, and be the quintessential monkey. His acrobatics were renowned, and tourists came to watch him flip around the trees.

One of my students was a tall, graceful woman, quiet in her manner and empathic. Years later I learned that she had become a physician. She spent her observation time totally immersed in the world of these monkeys. Not only did she try to understand their way of living, she wanted to go deeper; to penetrate their point of view, the *content* of their minds. To be a good observer, one must sit still, suspend oneself, and quiet one's mind. Somehow achieving this near meditative state allows something I can only call "flow" from one species to another; a comprehension *sans paroles*. Perhaps some ancient part of the brain responds to its equivalent. People were very attracted to Popeye, not only for his acrobatics, but because he had a quality of *maleness* without macho; of leadership without bullying, of gentleness without weakness.

Another one of my students was quite religious and decided to offer an orange to Popeye. He would be an incarnation of Hanuman, and the gift would be her token of respect. Popeye accepted this gift without grabbing or threatening (as some monkeys do even when food is proffered). Rather, in his judicious way, he calmly took it, peeled it and slowly enjoyed its sweetness. His apparent delight was a reflection or perhaps more accurately, a *projection* of the joy humans can take in simple pleasures. A few days before we were to leave, the tall student I mentioned earlier was sitting on a bench near a ravine, about to eat an apple when Popeye came up the cliff from beneath her position. Naturally she assumed he wanted the fruit, but he ignored it, and simply put his arms around her and hugged. While I gasped at this astonishing show of affection, this incredible interaction, she remained motionless, barely breathing. It seemed that Popeye had come up from the ravine for this purpose, that he *knew* she was there and came to be with her. Popeye stayed awhile not moving, seemingly wanting something from this contact. Sometime later he released her, and went off.

I never did get back to Kowloon after that field season. So I don't know what happened to Popeye. I keep the images, the lessons in mothering and leadership; the how-to-avoid-back-biting-while-grooming that I observed. I like to think of Popeye gaining leadership in his group, his judiciousness promoting him to that position, and his goodness protecting him from harm. I like to think of him aging gently, unperturbed by human action. Certainly his story and the other two may not prove that monkeys have profound feelings, but they surely intimate as much. My life changed because I knew them, felt them, was allowed to be amongst them. I have become—sometimes painfully—aware that other people do not recognize monkeys let alone dogs, cats, horses or rabbits as I do; that these mammals have all the basic needs, wants, feelings that move us. I accept that there are enormous differences of course, but somehow these only enhance what we have in common.

Frances Burton

# Part Four

## Friends Who Touch Our Lives and Our Hearts Forever

# How to Say "Respect" in Chinese

I want to tell you about one of my adventures in Taiwan but first a little bit about myself. I was raised on a farm in Nova Scotia. My Mom was eighteen when she gave birth to me, her daughter. Although she had only a grade six education, she is the wisest woman I've ever met. I grew up knowing that she loved me unconditionally just because I'm me.

After my children reached adulthood, I wanted to experience another part of the world and decided to go to Taiwan to teach ESL. I was incredibly fortunate to get a job at a very unique school called The Natural Way. Unlike most schools in China (which are primarily dreary, storefront facilities) this school was set on an acre of beautifully landscaped property. It had its own small farm and magnificently-designed buildings. The school accommodated pre-schoolers to grade six, and the upstairs of the

340

schoolhouse was a performing arts facility. My roommate, Teacher Vee, a feisty, elegant, redhead from South Africa (who became my life-long friend and soul mate) and I had the two pre-school classes in adjoining classrooms.

As most of you know, the Chinese culture has practised Collectivism for thousands and thousands of years; a culture where any behavior diverse or different from the cultural norms is ignored or ostracized. This way of life, combined with many learning inhibited conditions of the children, was not conducive with the school's mandate of teaching the love of learning.

In Teacher Vee's class, which adjoined mine, was a four-year-old boy named Little John. Little John was obviously autistic; he never interacted with the other children or the teachers and stood all day in a corner. Periodically he darted from one corner of the room to another. He never spoke and, of course, the children and teachers ignored him.

His mother brought a prognosis and treatment instructions from Little John's doctor. The medical people deducted that the reason Little John didn't speak was because his jaw muscles and lungs had never fully developed.- The teachers were instructed to make him chew bubble gum all day, and four times a day, they had to hold this little boy up against a wall with his feet dangling until he screamed. This was the remedy for his inability to speak. It was torturous for Teacher Vee and I to hear his screams and to be totally powerless to help this little man. When the treatments were done, Teacher Vee would hurry to comfort him and run his hands under the running water faucet, the only thing that seemed to soothe him.

Vee was beside herself with rage over this treatment and went to the school administration, to the authorities and to anyone else who would listen, to try to stop it. She begged the Chinese teachers to halt the treatments but they all ignored her efforts. I continuously encouraged her to try a different method. We couldn't change millions of years of culture by preaching; we had to show them that Little John was special. We both put extra effort and time involving him in play with the other children, reading quietly to him alone, speaking to him constantly and consistently, and comforting him after his "treatments."

One day many weeks later, Little John received particularly aggressive and traumatic "treatment." Teacher Vee left her classroom and came to me in tears of anguish and frustration. I hugged her and rocked her while she cried and promised that if she went for some air to calm herself, I'd wait close to Little John to give him comfort when the teachers had finished. When she left, our lead teacher, Teacher Kai approached me and asked why Teacher Vee was so upset. I explained that her heart was breaking because of Little John's terror. She asked me point blank if I thought Little John didn't speak because he was "special. This was a word only Vee and I used in describing John.

"Yes, absolutely," I said. "We have to love his specialness and who he is if he is ever to find quality of life and happiness in society."

By lunchtime everything had calmed down and we were helping to serve the pre-school children lunch in their common area. A sombre mood hung over the whole school that day. I noticed Little John leaving the table and making his way towards Teacher Vee; he held his empty bowel up to her and very clearly said, "More please, Teacher Vee." ……..his very first words and in English!

Sorry, but I still get tears in my eyes every time I hear that little voice saying those words in my head.

Teachers rushed to him with hugs. Vee and I jumped and cheered; the children also cheered. We could hear students in other classrooms cheering and shouting and realized that the news of Little John's first words had spread all over the school. Soon our area of the school filled with children and teachers from other classrooms. It was a joyous time and we nearly scared Little John half to death. He left the room.

Rapidly, many changes lead by Teacher Kai began to happen around the school. Beth (a grade six student with a hearing impairment) had her desk moved from the back of the classroom up to the front beside the teacher's desk. Minnie (a grade three student, visually impaired and with a severe learning disability) was given extra reading help, a straight-edge ruler to underline the words when she read and training in word processing for her writing activities. Horatio (a grade one student with ADHA) was provided with attention, quiet spaces and activities when he got out of control. Crystal (an introvert and one of my pre-schoolers who didn't talk very much but loved to sing) was offered special classes in vocals. Her mother or I always attended when she performed to help her overcome her shyness.

And John? Well John chose his own activities and was supported by both his fellow pupils and the administrative and teaching staff in his interactions. If he wanted to join grade three for story time or listen to the musicians practice or watch our secretary type, he was encouraged to do so and accepted. He liked to "teach" other children to read and they gave him all the patience and attention a little boy could take. And yes, his vocabulary grew!

This symbol of respect has come to be very meaningful to me after my experience with Little John and the transformation at The Natural Way. In the Chinese culture it has many meanings: courteous behavior, politeness, good manners, gratitude and even worship, but in general it means "a display of dignity in action." To me, this translates into honoring others for who they are, not what I want them to be. One thing I learned for sure: Little John and Mom taught me that respect and love know no boundaries.

She-she-ne-e (Thank you).

# Evelyn, the Good Mother

Imagine if you could have the ideal mother. What would she be like? Perhaps gentle, kind, nurturing, someone who would build your self-esteem, encourage your dreams and love you unconditionally. I was to find my ideal mother in a relationship that evolved over a period of thirty years.

I am not demeaning my biological mother, Ann. She did her best. In my forties I came to understand and sympathize with her. Ann had come of age during the Great Depression and its effects proved long-reaching. There was never enough money and she was anxious about saving and spending. That anxiety transferred to me. My teen years were tough because of the combination of her going through menopause and me trying to assert my independence under her constant stream of criticism. When I headed off to university only because I had won a scholarship, she commented, "Education is wasted on a girl;

you'll just get married." I see now that came from my harsh grandmother.

Mom called me "a baby" when at seventeen I complained of painful abdominal cramps. Before government-funded health insurance it cost money to see a doctor. Ten years later I was diagnosed with full blown endometriosis. I narrowly escaped a hysterectomy. When I had surgery to remove two large tumors from my ovaries, to her credit, my mother tended me during my recovery. The problem wasn't that she didn't care for me; it was her ignorance and fear.

The one gift Ann gave me was the joy of reading. I started school knowing how to read, a definite advantage, making school a breeze and teaching a natural career. Yes, I did marry. I also divorced and have supported myself my entire life.

How did I meet my "ideal mother?" That meeting occurred on a sunny afternoon in July, 1975 while visiting my parents in Prince Edward County where they had moved the preceding year.

"Gail, Evelyn has invited us for tea," Ann said. "Would you like to go?"

Evelyn, Ann and Frances formed a triumvirate. As young mothers, they had been friends when they lived in Pickering

Township in the fifties. They renewed their friendship in the early seventies when all three moved to "the county." Evelyn was the front runner, moving with her husband, Joe, to a summer retreat at a sprawling Victorian farmhouse on Big Island. It later became their permanent home. Frances and her husband, also named Joe, moved there a few years later, then my parents, Ann and John, to a bungalow in town.

I think synchronicity was at play here.

My father maneuvered the winding rural road until we reached Evelyn's home, a brown frame house with pink shutters, surrounded by poppies and pink peonies. A poem by Christina Rossetti springs to mind:
I wish I could remember the first day
First hour, first moment of your meeting me
So unrecorded did it slip away.

If I had known what would occur, perhaps I would have paid better attention. I can't recall much about Evelyn at our initial meeting as I was distracted by her tall, dark, son David with the green eyes. I was a naïve twenty-seven year old, two years divorced. Handsome David was twenty-three, a recent college graduate summering with his family before heading off to South Dakota for graduate studies in mining engineering. As "the adults" enjoyed tea, David played his acoustic guitar and sang folk songs to me.

It turned into a sweet summer romance. During the time I spent with David going to the beach or swimming at the dock, I came to know his parents over lunches, dinners, euchre games and singing round the piano as Evelyn played. I felt comfortable and accepted in this family. Even Joe, an Irish sparkle in his eyes said, "You're okay for a divorcee."

Joe and Evelyn had adopted three young boys when each was about four years old. David was their youngest and only surviving son. They had adopted Edward first, then Robert. They lost Robert to a devastating illness when he was eight and after grieving went on to adopt David. Edward died in a motorcycle accident in his thirties. Evelyn did not allow these tragedies to cloud her positive outlook. Edward's widow and daughters continued in a long and loving relationship with Evelyn. Parents and children find each other in this world; love isn't about biology.

My own nuclear family had gone through periods of closeness but never as portrayed by those nostalgic television shows of the fifties, although my father and

349

I did have a *Father Knows Best* relationship. I admired and loved him, and in return, he was kind and encouraging. We four–my mother, father, sister and me–were not a "happy family unit" although we tried. I have always longed to be part of a truly happy family and envious of those who live it so naturally.

Whenever I made the three-hour drive from Toronto to "the county," I would ask my mom if we could visit Evelyn. By now she and Joe had moved into the bungalow he built using stone instead of brick on the outside frame of the house. The house stood on a portion of their subdivided property. They had started building it that first summer I met them.

As we drove around the curve, I was drawn to the extensive gardens–a colorful rockery fronting the house and a large side garden in crimson and gold extending the length of the property to the lake. Deep red poppies, bright daisies and black-eyed Susans swayed in the breeze. (I still have butter yellow primroses blooming today, children of the first plant Evelyn gave me when I bought my house.)

Evelyn ran to meet us. Her soft blonde curls framed her delicate face and radiant smile. She wore a crisp cotton blouse in pastel yellow and a yellow and rose princess-line skirt which accentuated her petite form. Her outfit was set off by a single strand of pearls –her trademark. She had set her table with linens and fine china. The aroma of freshly- baked banana muffins and garden-picked raspberries filled the kitchen, and a delicate bouquet of flowers provided a centerpiece. This served as the setting to the kinship we shared. Today when I serve tea to friends it is on Real Old Blue Willow, my garden flowers adding to the ambience. I think this is a reflection of those many times with Evelyn. Unlike her, I do not bake, but the berries and carrot cake I purchase are still delicious. Sometimes we are unknowing role models.

I can't recall who started the letter writing; though I have a strong feeling it was Evelyn–first a paragraph or two in a Christmas card, then birthday and valentine cards. From there it expanded. We both chose cards and notepaper in pastel pinks or ripe with flowers. I have kept those precious letters.

I'd always sent post cards to my parents while traveling so included Evelyn. For her I sought out floral post cards– hibiscus from the Caribbean or lavender from Provence. At the Vatican in Rome I realized I could mail a card with their special stamp. Hers was the only address I knew by heart. I sent her Michelangelo's sculpture of the pieta and as she is religious, I am sure she liked it.

I wasn't her only writing companion. Evelyn kept up a regular correspondence with her sister Olive, daughter-in-law Nancy, granddaughters and friends. "Little chats on paper" she called them. Snapshots of a life, a way to share joy and sorrows, triumphs and everyday moments. Sometimes writing frees you and you'll say things in a letter you wouldn't say face to face. These thoughts and feelings emerge from the quiet of your heart.

I would write to her about my students, my travels, my latest sweetheart, descriptions of my garden and my anticipation of the first golden daffodils and regal delphiniums. She'd write about baking Nanaimo bars and lemon squares for Christmas, about her volunteer work in the nursing home and reading with school children, about visits with her son, my parents and her neighbors.

When my mother Ann moved into a nursing home, the bond with Evelyn strengthened. After visiting my mother, Evelyn wrote me about her progress. She wrote of the social coordinator taking Mom on a walk to get the mail and how "she very politely introduced me to her roommate–she was definitely with it today. She was in good spirits." My feisty, talkative mother suffered from vascular dementia as a result of a series of small strokes which eventually robbed her of speech and memory.

Evelyn's "reports" helped to assuage my guilt. A demanding teaching career made the six-hour round trip taxing. After we placed Mom in the retirement home my sister moved to Vancouver. This left me feeling responsible for my mother. It was in old age that my mother finally came to appreciate me.

One time when I called Margaret, the lady we had hired as Mom's caregiver, to bathe her and take her for ice cream and read to her, Evelyn mentioned that Mom said she missed me.

"She must have meant my sister," I said.

She replied "Your mother clearly said 'I miss Gail.' "

I felt so loved.

Evelyn and I mailed each other poetry. She found uplifting poems in books and copied them out to share with me. I'd call her a "practical romantic." Her life was grounded in reality but her heart looked to the stars. In this we were kindred spirits. I mailed her my creations. She believed in me as a writer, often when I doubted myself. She was thrilled when I started getting published, first poems in anthologies by the Canadian Authors Association, and later travel essays in newspapers and magazines.

One autumn day I offered Evelyn my arm as we crossed the road to lunch at Lake of the Mountain Inn. She blew me out of the water with her comment, "You know I've always thought of you as my daughter-in-law."

I can't recall what I wrote to her that January of 1998 when her beloved Joe passed away. Perhaps I shared my own shock and grief at my father's passing and its effect on me. I didn't attend Joe's funeral but did arrange for my mother to go accompanied by a nurse from the Victorian Order of Nurses. Whatever I wrote reached across the wintry miles and comforted her. It was touching the way she opened her heart.

In a letter to me, she wrote, "Your beautiful letter was more than sympathy; it was empathy–you have been there. I will keep your letter and feast on it now and again. The tears well up easily and in unexpected places."

354

When my mother Ann passed away in May 1, 2003, the bond between Evelyn and I grew tighter. I had taken both mothers, two old friends, out to tea on many visits and now I started sending flowers to Evelyn on the occasions I had sent them to my mother– Christmas, birthday, Easter. When I visited "the county," my second home, I stopped at a florist for a fresh bouquet and brought Kit Kat chocolate bars or ice cream. Evelyn and I would have a little party in her room in later years when she was living in a nursing home and had become too frail to go on outings. I had done this for both my parents.

On October 17, 2005, Evelyn turned ninety. I'd like to think I orchestrated the celebration or was at least a catalyst. After too many years I called David and asked what he was planning for his Mom's birthday.

"Should we be doing something?" he asked.

Men!

"I think she'd like an 'at home'– people dropping by to extend wishes and share tea and treats."

Evelyn said she didn't "want a fuss." The retirement home staff who cherished her and the second generation of the triumvirate pitched in to make it a fitting soiree, down to the balloons and piano music.

On her ninetieth birthday, Evelyn greeted guests in the main living room with a brilliant smile, quiet joy and stalwart acceptance of life. Perhaps it was her faith; perhaps it was her closeness to the earth as a gardener that made her aware of life's important moments. With poise she blew out her candles and reminded us all, "Today is the first day of the rest of your life." She had read the quote and made it her own.

Without realizing it, Evelyn was a mother figure and mentor. She combined wisdom and youth in one human being for she both accepted and rejoiced in life. Despite illness, loss and adversity, she never lost her sense of wonder. It showed in the quiet grace of her smile and it appeared in her letters.

Mid-July of 2009, I received an email from David in Arizona where he lived half of the year. He wrote that his mother was in hospital. It sounded serious.

"I thought you might want to know as you and my mother have a special relationship," he said in the email.

I phoned the florist for a large bouquet of red roses, roses I wish I had sent in the spring when she was still vital. You see Evelyn had stopped writing due to her Parkinson's and broken arm. I kept writing to her though, I needed to. No one had let me know of her condition and that she had started to fail that spring. It is the one regret I have in our relationship.

When I arrived at the hospital I found that she had been moved that morning to a nursing home. On a hunch I stopped by the retirement home. I found David there organizing her things for the move. He filled me in, which helped to ease the shock when I saw her. From him I learned of all the physical trials and illness she'd never talked about. Despite all that we shared, she was a private person in some respects and never one to burden or complain as some elderly people do.

When I walked into the nursing home, she smiled and reached her hand out to me. She didn't know my name but she knew there was love and trust between us. David sat on one side of her and I sat on the other, each of us holding one of her hands. I sensed she was a little frightened. My words and presence seemed to offer comfort and sustenance to them both. We had come full circle.

When I returned the next day, I took Evelyn out to the sunny patio and showed her the plants. She was distracted as she fiddled with cards and letters. I tried to read some to her but she drifted off. She was already crossing over. I sensed it would be the last time I would see her.

David stayed by her side the next few weeks. His new wife was waiting for him in Wisconsin. I was thankful that he hadn't brought his wife and could devote all of his attention to his mother.

Evelyn passed away August 7; 2009.We had met when she was a resilient sixty. I offered to speak at her service. The night before her service, David and I talked over dinner with Gord and Monika. Gord is Frances' youngest son. David had been staying with them since Evelyn's illness and I was welcomed to their home on my visits. The second generation had quite naturally carried on the friendship of the first. We spoke of happy memories and laughter filled the air during that dinner. Later David shared with me a white journal he had given to his mother.

"Mom wrote in it for forty years," he said. "I thought we could read some aloud during the service."

There in tiny perfect script were pages of poems, inspirational sayings and affirmations.

I'd like to think Evelyn was looking down on us that afternoon in the little Methodist church filled with friends and family, poetry and music–surely her spirit was with us. David was tearful as he spoke of Evelyn; her sister Olive made us smile as she talked about how she envied her curls and how as little girls they had giggled together, and I spoke of things we had shared. I was fine until the organ music started and David whispered to me, "The family will follow the coffin." I was part of the family and realized in that moment I had lost another mother.

That night David handed me an envelope. He had discovered it while going through her things. She had written and addressed it back in March but not mailed it. The note on the card had taken her a few sittings and the script was difficult to read. I sense she had labored over it.

It seemed a farewell. The card itself depicted a garden with roses, delphiniums and daisies. She wrote:

"You have been so faithful in correspondence and gift-wise. The flowers have all been beautiful and the nice cards!

Thank you so much for remembering me. The flowers on this card remind me of you Gail…..you are a true friend. Much love you forever and ever."

I kept her alive a little longer by writing a piece for Lives Lived in *The Globe and Mail*. It gave me closure. In order to complete the submission guidelines I had to fill in the first sixty years of her life by interviewing her ninety-two-year-old sister Olive. I learned of her girlhood and the sweet story of how she met her beloved Joe. Although a top student, she left high school at sixteen to work as a nanny and moved to Calgary with her young charges. At twenty-two, she returned for her sister's wedding and met Joe who was a family friend and "the boy next door." They married in 1941, the same year as my parents and the height of World War II.

Olive and I enjoyed reminiscing that night. Evelyn had done so much for me. I wanted to share her remarkable spirit with the wider world. Publishing the piece also affirmed her belief in me as a writer and left a keepsake for her granddaughters.

On February 14, 1999, I'd found a valentine card that touched a chord with both of us. I know because Evelyn wrote how much she liked the quote:

Certain friendships come to be
Not by chance but destiny.

Evelyn nurtured people much the way she tended her garden and I consider myself fortunate to have been one of them. A relationship is like a perennial garden–it develops over time; as the soil is amended the plants flourish and mature.

Evelyn lived a life of grace, dignity and quiet humility. Our lives touched and resonated and we were both the better for it.

# Frenchie

When I was growing up I had an unusual friend for a little girl. He was one of the town drunks. My grandfather owned a tavern in a small coal mining town in southern Illinois and Frenchie was one of his better patrons. Sometimes my grandfather kicked Frenchie out of the tavern because he was too intoxicated and my grandfather wouldn't serve him anymore. I always liked him when he was drunk because then he sometimes played hopscotch with me, which he wouldn't do when he was sober.

At the age of two, my mother and I had come to live with my grandparents. Frenchie said that the first time he saw me I was sitting on a pool table, playing with some toys and jabbering away, so he called me Blabberbox. It stuck as his name for me.

To me, Frenchie was a wonderful person, a bit quirky, certainly different from what most people would consider a reasonable companion to a child, but he clearly liked me and made me feel special.

Maybe our relationship was a novelty for him in some ways. He reportedly had been abusive toward his wife and his own children and they had moved away before I knew him. Perhaps I represented a grandchild who would make no demands and for whom he had no responsibility. Whatever the reason, it was obvious that our friendship brought him pleasure. I never questioned his friendship. For me, it was a constant.

My mother didn't approve of my relationship with Frenchie; she was not happy about it at all. In retrospect, I think perhaps part of her disapproval had to do with her belief that because Frenchie was a drunk he would reveal family secrets. However, he never did because he had great loyalty to me.

I think that my mother's strong feelings against him made me like Frenchie even more. I also had strong, but vague feelings; however; mine stemmed from thinking I was an outsider and perhaps believing something about me was off for some reason. Frenchie and I really liked each other. Perhaps we intuitively realized we were kindred spirits. Because I was withdrawn and ill at ease with people, no one really knew me very well and no one appeared to know the Frenchie I knew. They just saw him as a drunk.

Although my mother seemed to think he would be a bad influence; in his way, Frenchie was always protective of me. His standard attire was bib overalls, usually in the summertime without a shirt underneath. Sometimes he wore a T-shirt. On his shoulder, he had a tattoo of a naked woman named Neva. When I was a little kid I always wanted to look at this tattoo. In those days you didn't see such things on television or in books. When he saw me looking, he either covered it over with his hand or pulled his shirt sleeve down.

Our town was poor, so Frenchie, like many of the miners, lived in houses with no plumbing or central heating–our house didn't have an indoor toilet until I was about ten. What money he had, he generally drank away. Men in those days were "tough" and not very demonstrative. But, once, when I was small, my grandpa brought home a teddy bear from the tavern. He said that Frenchie bought it for me as a Christmas present. I was very proud and fond of this teddy bear. My mother was not happy about this gift and made derogatory comments about how it had probably come into his possession. Then my teddy bear disappeared. For years I blamed my mother and accused her of stealing it because she didn't like Frenchie. She denied this, but I believed it was true and often threw it up to her. When she moved house after more than thirty years in one place, my mother found my teddy bear in the last box she checked in the attic. She grabbed my teddy, and waved it triumphantly as she came downstairs, happy to prove that she was innocent of my allegations. However, she never denied disliking Frenchie.

For several years we continued to live with my grandparents and I was very, very attached to them. Once we moved away, we visited often and I spent a lot of time there in the summers. When I went to university and then out of the country, I naturally saw less and less of Frenchie.

After my grandmother died I went home. Where I come from, a wake and a funeral are very important social occasions and not attending is considered extremely disrespectful. Frenchie didn't come to the visitation or the funeral. Everyone said this was probably because he was on a drunk. I insisted that if Frenchie had known he would have been there. After the burial everyone went back to the house and I said I was going to see Frenchie. People muttered and rolled their eyes, but off I went anyway.

I found him at the side of his house gathering wood for his stove. At this time he was well into his seventies, and he had very bad cataracts. He didn't recognize me, and I startled him.

"Who's there?" he asked.

"It's Janice," I said.

"Blabberbox, why are you here? It's January. You're not supposed to be here now."

"My grandma died. That's why I'm here."

"I don't believe it. I didn't know. Oh Janice, I'm so sorry. If I would have known I would have come. You know I would have come, but I was in Indiana at my son's house, and I didn't know."

We went into the house, talked for a while, and came back outside. I returned home and defiantly told my family why Frenchie hadn't been at the funeral.

"Oh, he probably wouldn't have come anyway," my mother said.

One of my uncles stared at me.

"I wonder how it feels, Janice," he said. "You really like Frenchie, but everyone always says these terrible things about him."

366

I so much appreciated that statement.

That was the last time I saw Frenchie. When he died, my mother didn't call me. I found out when a card I had sent him came back with *Deceased* written on it. I called my mother, angry that she hadn't told me he had died. I wanted to go to the funeral but she said she didn't know for sure when he had died or even if there was to be a funeral.

The next time I went home, I found out where he was buried and my aunt and I went to look for his grave. The area near our home has three cemeteries, so we visited each of them, walking up and down rows trying to locate his burial spot. Eventually we found someone who worked in the cemetery and he was able to show us the family plot. It contained a big stone with the name of Frenchie's brother and his parents, but there was no stone for Frenchie. There was no acknowledgement at all of Frenchie's existence. I bought him a stone. It only has one word, *Frenchie*. Frenchie used to tell everyone, "Blabberbox always sends me a card for everything.

She sends me cards for Christmas and Easter and Halloween. She even sends me a card for Groundhog's Day."

Sometimes, when I visit his grave and I see that gravestone, it is like I've sent him a card.

# The Miracle

My friend David married June and at age thirty-three June became pregnant. Because David and I were close, I shared his joy, even though children weren't part of my life. When June was twenty-three weeks pregnant she began to continually vomit and suffer horrible headaches. At first, she thought it might be that she'd caught some bug, but she was sent home from the hospital emergency on March 30 after she was able to keep down some food.

After this procedure, she came home. She was all right for a while, but then she started feeling unwell, and developed several symptoms: throwing up all the time, blurry vision, hallucinating and violent headaches which became progressively worse. On April 1, David phoned the doctor.

"Something is happening here," David said.

"Well, she's pregnant," the doctor replied. "It could be because of that."

Over the next few hours June's symptoms became much worse so David called an ambulance and took her back to the hospital.

"Something is wrong here," he said to the doctor. "Even her eyesight is going."

"We don't know what it could be," the doctor replied.

"Well, check everything. Check the shunt."

A shunt had been inserted in June's head three years earlier when doctors diagnosed her with Chiari malformation, a defect in the lower rear of the skull that blocks the flow of cerebrospinal fluid. Her parents thought the problem might be the shunt.

June stayed at the hospital overnight and a CT scan showed the shunt was working. She went home the next day but started to hallucinate so David took her back to the hospital on April 4.

They did another CT scan to check the shunt again and found it was faulty on both ends so, on April 8, they replaced it and within one hour June was fine. The doctors decided to keep June in the hospital overnight just for observation because it was now late in the evening anyway.

The next day I received a frantic phone call from David. He said that at one o'clock in the morning, the doctor at the hospital had called him.

"Can you come in?" the doctor had asked. "We have bad news for you. Your wife cannot breathe on her own. We've got her on life support actually." They had done so because of her pregnancy.

During the night June had climbed out of bed, forgetting she had a catheter, fallen down and hit her head, vomited and aspirated into her lungs. She suffered complete respiratory arrest. Because of lack of oxygen, damage occurred to both sides of the brain.

"We'll monitor the baby and see if it's going to be all right," the doctors had said to David on June 15. "We'll try to bring the baby as close to term as possible by keeping June on life support for four more weeks. As soon as we birth the baby we'll have to take June off life support and let her go."

David had no choice but to go along with it. I tried to comfort him the next day when we met. But there was little I could do except listen and be there for him.

June was in a coma on life support for five weeks, clinically dead. Then something strange happened. June revived. One day she opened her eyes and moved her arm. The doctors still can't explain it.

"This is a miracle," the doctor said. "It doesn't happen."

The effects of the damage to June's brain made it impossible for her to walk without any support or speak and think clearly. She does not have normal use of her body. Almost three years later she still lives in a hospital room. Sometimes she can get words out. She knows what she's trying to say but can't always achieve it. She points to lists of words.

Diana, the baby, was born one month premature, but very healthy. We hadn't known what she would be like. Her daddy, David, had asked me a few months before her birth, "If the baby is all right when she is born would you like to be her godfather?"

"David, I really don't want that responsibility," I replied.

I didn't at the time. I was a free spirit, very independent. Because I work in the theatre, it was common for me to take off at a moment's notice. I didn't particularly relate to kids and used to say, "It's all right to have kids as long as you can afford to have somebody look after them for you."

"I just thought I'd ask because I'd really have liked you to," David said.

David brought Diana to me after they discharged her from the hospital at twelve days old. We were sitting in my living room, and he was giving her a bottle.

"Why don't you take her for a bit and give her the bottle?" he asked.

I hesitated a bit.

"Oh, all right then, fine."

He put her on my knee and I gave her the bottle. She started staring at me, and I looked at her. The thought came into my mind. *I think I love you, I really do.* I don't know what it was, but Diana and I had an immediate bond. It was a very loving spiritual connection, soul to soul.

After a few hours, David took her home and I started thinking about her and the situation, asking myself, *What's David going to do? How is he going to manage? How is he going to look after the baby when he has to work during the day?*

The next day he brought the baby again.

"Let's look after the baby between us as much as we can," I said.

"I was hoping you'd feel that way. Okay, let's bring her up."

I thought, *Yes, my life will change.* However, I didn't care because this experience and this love were the important factors. *When I work in theater I can usually arrange it so I can go in at night. It's going to be hard, but I'll do it.* And I did.

David brings Diana to me around ten in the morning and picks her up around four. I have her all day and go into work around 5:30 in the evening.

The first days with Diana were an adjustment. In the beginning when she needed a bottle or changing she would yell the place down. One day, when she did this, I laid her on the bed, took her diaper off and she peed all over me. I completely panicked. She was wet and I was soaking. That was a learning experience. I haven't panicked since.

It's been an incredible experience that keeps evolving with great love and affection. I just adore her. When she started calling me *Dada*, I said, "No, Uncle Tony." I didn't want her getting mixed up. She calls me *Uncle Tony* now.

I see her change every day. She's very tuned into things. She loves music, dancing, acting, drawing, painting, and can play the CD player herself, not bad for a two-year-old. She just picks up words and uses them in context. She's very bright, extremely affectionate, never gets depressed, and is very happy.

David takes Diana to see her mother every day. When he leaves here at the end of the afternoon, he goes directly to the hospital. They stay with June for an hour or so. Diana gives her a big kiss and sits on the bed with her.

What a different space I'm in now to the one I was in before I met Diana. She's a handful, actually two handfuls, but when she isn't around I miss her. I feel a strong relationship with her, almost as a father to a daughter. I feel very protective towards her. David and I absolutely adore her. We talk about her all the time.

"Isn't she beautiful!" we say. "Isn't she gorgeous! She's so clever!"

Diana is now two years and four months old. She's very bright. Last week I took her to the museum. I told her they had dinosaurs there.

"Oh, I don't want to go see the dinosaurs," she said.

"Why?" I asked.

"They might bite me."

In the museum we saw a replica of a furnished Renaissance bedroom. Harpsichord music was playing and Diana began to dance. Other museum visitors stood and watched while she continued to dance. She was performing. She's not shy at all.

After three hours in the museum I was exhausted, but she didn't want to leave. She loved it.

I hope that I will always have her around but figure that maybe I won't. I'll forever be concerned for her to the point of worrying. For example, when she catches a little cold, I worry. I know our strong loving connection will continue, but whether or not I will see her to the degree I see her now, I don't know. However, I don't want to think or project that about the future. When she isn't around, I miss her something awful. I just love her.

Tony Moffat-Lynch

# Julian

Sometime in the mid-1980s I was invited to a Fourth of July party given by a friend of mine on Nantucket. At this big party, I met a nineteen-year-old man named Julian, and we became friends. As I was considerably older, old enough to be his grandmother, I was very much a mentor to him. Julian had recently graduated from the Fashion Institute of Technology and he had dreams and ambitions. He was a very hard-working boy. When other guys his age went dancing and drinking in discotheques and bars, Julian stayed home and worked on his portfolio. That was all he did.

He dreamt about working in Europe and traveled to Paris and Milan to find work there. In Milan he met with a famous designer who looked at his portfolio and invited Julian to come and work for him.

At this time I was in Venice, and Julian came to see me there.

"I've got something to tell you," he said. "I've taken a job in Milan."

It was a case of "be careful what you wish for" situation because then Julian was faced with the necessity of moving there.

When the day came for us to leave we went down to the dock. He took the vaporeta to the train station because he was going to Milan and I took the vaporeta to the airport as I was continuing on to London.

To my surprise, after a few days Julian showed up in London.

"What's the matter?" I asked him.

"I can't get anyone to tell me how much they're going to pay me. They're treating me like a young, Italian apprentice; I'm not. I'm an American designer. They're not treating me well, and I'm just not going to put up with it."

*This kid's got a lot of nerve* I thought,

"I'm a genius," he said.

I wanted to slap him.

"You can't go around saying you're a genius," I said. "That's for other people to say."

Julian traveled on to Paris and back to New York with me. In London and Paris the designer's office kept calling and Julian coolly ignored the calls and said, "I'll deal with it when I get back to New York." He wanted the security of being in the United

States and not a convenient train ride from Paris to Milan. He was extremely wise for his age. When we were both back in New York I heard him on the phone.

"If you want me to come to Milan, you must pay my airfare," he said. "You've got to tell me how much you're going to pay me and find me somewhere to live."

I couldn't believe Julian had this kind of strength and determination. They accepted his terms.

The night before he was to leave for Milan I found him crying in his room.

"Look, Julian," I said. "Don't make the mistake I made when I came to America from Europe. I thought I'd never see home again. It was ridiculous. I was back within a year visiting my family and every year since. If you don't like it just treat it like a holiday. There are certain bridges in life we must cross. I know it's comfortable for you here with your family and your friends, but if you don't do it, there will come a time when you will regret it and will hate yourself for it. My advice is that you go and then if you're unhappy in six months you come back."

The next morning he left for Milan.

They found him somewhere to live, paid him a salary and he went to work with the famous couturier. He made wonderful friends and found himself a beautiful apartment. On winter weekends he went skiing in Klosters, Switzerland and in summer spent time in St. Tropez. Both locations were accessible from Milan. He blossomed very much as a person. Julian visited me on Nantucket over the summer and he always returned to visit his family and me at Christmas.

In 1989, Julian started to get sick. He was twenty-six. A friend of his called from Milan and said he had collapsed and been diagnosed with epilepsy. He became seriously ill and when he came home at Christmas I could hardly recognize him. He never returned to Milan to work again.

Julian was put in the hospital for tests. He tested positive for AIDS. I was waiting in the corridor outside his hospital room when the doctor arrived with the results and informed me. I began to weep, and the doctor went into the room. He returned and said Julian wanted me to be in the room when he received the prognosis. I knew I couldn't let him see me like this. So I dried my eyes, changed my expression and braced myself for the performance I was about to give. I entered the room, sat down on the bed, and he held my hand. When the doctor told him, Julian gasped and began to cry. Without missing a beat, I immediately chimed in.

"This is wonderful news. You've spent months being treated for epilepsy. We've lost all this time. Now we know what can be done and we're going to fight this. You're going to get better. There's no shame in this. There's only shame if you think there's shame."

I made up my mind then and there that I was going to be Julian's strength. Anyone who has ever been a caregiver for someone who is terminally ill knows, it was a very demanding situation. Every day brought a different symptom to deal with, different medications, new procedures–and some of them were horrible. It was a rollercoaster of emotions. If he was having a scary procedure that day I stopped by the hospital in the morning before going to the office. When he wouldn't eat the hospital food I went there at lunch time and brought him food I knew he would like. I returned again in the evening, brought him dinner and stayed there until they rang the bell for visitors to leave. It was exhausting.

After several weeks, the doctors told me Julian would only last for about two more weeks. I carefully observed Julian and told the doctors that I thought they were wrong and, happily, as it turned out, they were wrong. He lived for another five years. When he left the hospital he resembled a skeleton. I took him to my house on Nantucket along with a young male nurse, David, who had been very kind to Julian in the hospital. They were about the same age. I watched Julian put on weight, four pounds in the first weekend when he dined on milkshakes and grilled cheese sandwiches at a popular luncheonette at the seaside resort. Once I found David crying.

"What's wrong?" I asked him.

"I just read Julian's history: he said. "He's going to die."

I told David that with his chosen vocation, this was something he must come to terms with and to know that he was helping Julian right now when he needed the support. Julian continued to gain weight and feel better.

Julian had extraordinary taste. Nothing was really quite good enough for him. He wanted the best and the most expensive and that's what he thought about everything. There was no substitute for quality. Naturally, he wanted to live on Fifth Avenue.

One late, winter afternoon as the light faded, and I walked my dog to the vet, I passed an apartment building on the next block to mine. A sign stood in front of it– "Apartment for Rent." It was something that you never saw in New York in those days when apartments went for a premium. The apartment was charming with a wood-burning fireplace flanked by bookcases and sconces on either side. Light from windows in every room, including the kitchen, filled the apartment. The bedroom overlooked a lovely garden. It was a unique and wonderful apartment. Julian looked at it and liked it.

I called the leasing agent who said she hadn't received a check from the person who wanted it.

"If you send a check over it's yours," she said.

I sent a check by messenger with Julian reimbursing me later. He asked if I wanted to get rid of him because he was staying in my guest room.

"No, Julian," I said. "While you're staying here, you are a victim. You must have your own apartment with your own things around you."

"Then I'll be a lonely victim," he replied.

I assured him that he could keep the key to my apartment, and, if he ever felt lonely or threatened or ill he could come back to the apartment. The guest room would always be made up and ready for him.

At this point, Julian had gone to see an equally prominent New York designer who had always wanted Julian to work with him. He hired Julian as a consultant. Julian had to go in to work only when the designer himself was in the office for design meetings. He was paid a generous salary. When Julian told me the news he was crying.

"Why?" I asked him.

"I'm doing this sick. Imagine what I could achieve if I were well."

It was all very heartbreaking. He had sprung back to life from death's door. He had a great job, a great apartment. Silently, we both knew he had limited time.

When he was diagnosed, I had prayed to God. *Please spare him.* It was a miracle. He had turned around. He had put on weight and looked the picture of health. People would ask me, "Is he really sick?" On holidays he went back to Switzerland to ski in the winter, and St. Tropez with his friends in the summer. When he first got out of the hospital, he'd seen a boy surfing. "I'll never be able to do that again," he sighed wistfully. Now he was surfing again.

While I was visiting friends in Maine he called me one day.

"I've had a terrible accident," he said.

"Oh, what's happened," I asked.

"I fell when I was surfing and cut my head on a rock. I had to go to the hospital and be stitched up."

"That's fantastic!" I said.

"What's fantastic about that?" he asked.

"Julian, you thought you'd never be able to surf again, and here you are surfing. I think that's great!"

The day came when he was moving out of my apartment to go live in his own. On that day, he delivered to me an etching by Canaletto (I told you he had great taste) of the Maria Salute in Venice. It's a beautiful church. We had seen it many times from the terrace of the Gritti Palace Hotel. I read the letter accompanying the painting. It said, *Thank you for the best year of my life.*

I stared at Julian, quizzically.

"The best year of your life?" I asked.

"Yes," he replied. "You taught me there are no negatives, only positives."

When Julian first became sick he went to Milan to pack up his apartment because he figured he was going home to die. Now he had a better apartment in New York, worked at a career he loved, and was with his friends. He had a wonderful life–looking healthy and robust, working and traveling.

One day I received a call. Julian had collapsed at the gym and was in the hospital. I went to see him. He removed his watch and his ring and gave them to me. Within a day he was in a coma and had brain damage.

"If he lives, he will never be able to dress himself or feed himself," the doctor said.

Once again, I prayed to God.

Before he lost his ability to speak, Julian took my hand and spoke words to me he had never said before.

"I love you, I love you so."

Those were the last words I ever heard him speak. That was fifteen years ago. He was thirty-one years old. I think of him every day

# Part Five

# Love, Love and More Love

# Frances Steloff

My husband was the President of Skidmore College. Literary people were in and out of our home all the time. On one of these occasions a mutual friend who loved books said, "You must meet Frances Steloff, a native of Saratoga Springs, a book lover and a book everything. She is the legendary book seller in all of New York and well beyond New York. She owns the Gotham Book Mart. She was the one who introduced James Joyce to American life and really defended him when he was quite controversial."

If you met or saw Frances Steloff on a street in New York City you might think she was a bag lady. She was tiny, very unprepossessing in appearance, with a pile of white hair. She must have been in her eighties or nineties when I first met her.

Frances hailed from the same town as I, Saratoga Springs, New York. Saratoga Springs is known for its famous race course. People come from all over during the racing season, and many stay at the grand hotels in town. Frances had grown up in a poor family. She was so poor she couldn't afford to buy shoes. As a child, she loved books, but couldn't have them. She left school in the fifth grade to help support her family. To earn money as a young woman in the early 1900s, Frances made the round of hotels to sell flowers to the guests. Sometimes she was barefoot.

At twenty she went to live with a cousin in Brooklyn. She worked in the corset department of Loeser's Department store. One December, the store's management asked her to take care of the Christmas book table. She enjoyed it so much that for the next twelve years she worked in several bookstores in New York. By her early twenties, her career, her life's work had begun.

In 1920, at the age of thirty-three she opened a bookstore, The Gotham Book Mart, in Manhattan. She was only able to stay there a few years. She bought the building at 51 West 47th St. and moved the store there. Behind this bookstore in the heart of the theatre district there was a backyard, not even landscaped, with some chairs. Here, she held gatherings with many interesting people, including authors Gertrude Stein, J.D. Salinger and Dylan

Thomas, from the United States, England, and other countries. Besides authors, many theatre people, poets and artists like Salvador Dali came to the store to meet Frances. She was very famous. I've seen photos of gatherings in the back of the store, and everyone you could imagine from the theatre would be sitting there on stools. Frances had posted these photos all over the store. You could name almost any author and he or she would have been a guest of hers in that backyard.

Everything sold was on consignment. She received most of the proceeds and anything left unsold was returned to the publishers. At that time it was a very unusual way to operate. Because she had grown up without books she had a passion for them and a real empathy for authors.

In her career, Frances fought against writing censorship. When the works of writers such as D. H. Lawrence and Henry Miller were banned she sold their books under the counter. She was harassed by the New York Society for the Suppression of Vice and received several summonses to appear in court. She thought censorship was nonsense and was proud to make those books available.

Frances became a rare book dealer, especially books out of print. It was incredible. In the back reaches of this little store you'd think no one could ever find anything because books were piled all over the floor in a hopeless mess. However, she knew every book's location, and she had one helper. She lived very modestly with two cats above the store. After twenty-three years at that address she later moved the store to 41 West 47th St.

I visited Frances when I was in New York and I remember seeing Marianne Moore there, wearing her tri-cornered hat and autographing her poetry books. I looked at these two old women, drinking their carrot juice together (both vegetarians). I felt so in awe that this most distinguished poet wrapped the books herself to mail to some of her readers who had asked for autographed copies. She was schlepping them to the post office, not using a stock boy in the bookshop.

"If they care that much about my work, the least I can do is autograph and mail it back to them," she said.

I found it very touching that these two marvelous, modest and unprepossessing women were so deeply passionate about books.

When she came to Saratoga Springs, Frances usually stayed with me. I think that the great lure wasn't me, but my dogs. She loved animals, and I had two great big poodles and a cat. They knew instinctively that she just loved them. They would sit outside her bedroom door and wait for her to come out.

We were friends. She made sure we would see each other whenever I was in New York. She would invite me to have lunch or, at least, come into her bookstore for a chat, which I gladly did.

When she died in 1989 at age 101, I wasn't able to go to the funeral service for her, a simple Jewish one. She'd asked to be buried in Saratoga Springs.

Everyone in New York who knew anything about books was familiar with the Gotham Book Mart. I discussed Frances with several people in the book business and we decided that she never read any of the books. I realized this because she wasn't able to discuss the books. When I shared my belief with others, I found that they had come to the same conclusion.

Frances Steloff's great contribution, her great love, was caring so deeply about the idea of books and supporting authors.

# French Fries

Every summer as a kid I would spend time with my grandparents. They lived in a lumber camp called Island Lake in Northern Ontario, about a six-hour drive from my home. The interesting thing about childhood memories is their limited scope of the real events, though I think most of our memories are tinted with our own personal selection.

There are two things I remember most vividly from those wonderful times, especially with my grandmother. I remember being at her house for the whole summer. I also remember feasting on her special homemade French fries every day for lunch.

Years later, when reminiscing with my mother about how fabulous it was to spend the whole summer in Island Lake, she stopped me. She laughed and said I would only go for one or two weeks. I was absolutely shocked. I could have sworn I spent a much longer time there.

The most amazing revelation was about the French fries. I have since come to discover that I was so very homesick every time I went. I was practically inconsolable. In her infinite wisdom, my grandmother discovered the one easy fix to put a smile on my face–homemade French fries. Just the idea of eating them made me happy as a kid.

My grandmother is long gone, yet my love for her is still as deep as ever. I also have continued my love affair with French fries to this day.

The interesting thing is that for the last five years or so I have complained about how they do not taste as good as I remember. I have continually experimented to create my own best fry, as well as sampling them wherever I get the chance. Somehow something always seems missing. I know, you think it's because Granny isn't making them. No, that's not it at all. You have to understand that I have been growing, learning and deliberately expanding my understanding of life and my spirituality. I have gradually come to realize that I am in complete control of my reactions to life. I know now that sometimes stuff happens, yet I am always in control of me, my emotions, my thoughts and my reactions. I am more self-empowered than I have ever been in my life. I have made the transition from spiritual practice to living spiritual principle most of the time. If I get caught up in some drama– (which I do occasionally), I remember this a lot sooner than I used to.

So it makes sense that French fries don't taste the way that I remember. I discovered, after much contemplation, that I ate French fries as a way of soothing my pain, sadness, and fear. Yet, in retrospect, I only consumed a pile of empty calories and my problems still remained. I have eaten them throughout most of my adult life to get through my stuff. Now I know it's the aware choices I continually make that soothe and empower me. I have always had the power to choose, I just wasn't taught how and when to do it in an empowering way.

It is my love for myself, my worthiness, the pursuit of my dreams and passions that get me through the difficult times. The crunchy little fry doesn't have that power.

The reason the French fries don't taste as good anymore is because they aren't the answer to what might be bothering me. Only I can decide what I can do to love myself enough to get through the hurdles without trying to push them away.

Maybe one day I will discover that perfect French fry. This time I know it will be because the fry is really good and not because I need soothing from an outside source for a challenge I might be experiencing.

Anne Ahokangas

## An 'I Love You' Lament

On hearing an 'I Love You' tossed into a
cell phone as a sign-off.
"Love, what is love?" as Prince Charles
once famously asked.

For me, love means people, although
I know you can love books, dogs, cats,
donuts, handbags and the sight of flying
mackerel. You can 'love' travel, tapestry,
trifle and ancient history. I accept that. But
I'm with the royal, wondering what Love
really means, especially when it comes to
the modern habit of tossing it into a
communication device held tight to the ear.
I'm utterly baffled by this 'sign off' to be
heard day and night on street corners, at bus
stops and in supermarket aisles.

What happened to, "See you soon,"
"Bye," and "Ciao!" What happened to
shrinking into a corner, dodging behind a
tree or melting into the night, when
something personal is underway?

These days, anywhere and
everywhere, it's, "Hi, did you want a large
packet of peas or a small one? I Love You."
Or "I'll be late, Honey, don't worry. Love
you." Even "I never! Swear. Look, home
soon and we'll go walkies. Love you."

Are these folk addressing a spouse, a young girl or a dog? That not being clear, plus the casual tone, trivializes the three most potent words in the universe. Heck, three 'I Love You's' should last a life time! One for youth, a second for mid-life and a spare for old age—a just-in-case. These need to be used sparingly, handled like fledglings, guarded like gold. Cell-phone junkies are squandering their inheritance every day—spendthrifts, the lot.

I want to yell, "Stop! Don't waste priceless words on check-ins. Treasure them like virginity. Please thank which ever deity you believe in, and hang on to your riches like grim death." Have you no other words, no better way of sorting daily trivia? Bandied words are lost words; commonplace and valueless.

And I don't think ILYs should be wasted on children. If kids don't know they're loved when they're treated with slavish patience, fed twice a day, dressed in designer clothes, loaded with electronic gadgets and sleep in queen-sized beds…tough!

I Love You's are for lovers. For whispering hoarsely on starlight nights so shot with silver you can see life on six planets; for mountain tops whose views beggar belief, for magnolia gardens when you're caught in a pair of arms, and so aflame with desire, you can smell your clothes singeing, for beaches where the salt-tinged spume of pounding rollers matches your heartbeat. ILYs are meant for occasions when clout is called for. I cringe hearing people bankrupt themselves, whispering to an airhead they've only known a couple of months, a dolly bird they met half an hour ago. Don't get me wrong, I love the love words, just not when they're kidnapped for inconsequential usage and tossed out like confetti.

   I was once tempted to cash in my last one. He was a younger co-worker, mysterious, with a soft, caressing voice. My husband had been working away for a long time. At a party, on a patio after a slow dance and I found myself still in his arms, inhaling the musky smell of his shirt, absorbing the wonder of a dragon's-back of mountain ridges lit by a blue moon—a strike-the-gong moment. I was saved from perdition by the stupidest of chances.

   Looking up at the face of my would-be lover in the opalescent light, I spotted a rosy swelling at the corner his perfect mouth. The tell-tale sign of an incipient cold sore. I hesitated and backed away. A cool breeze blew between us. I swallowed, coughed, muttered that I needed the bathroom and slipped inside.

So, years on, I still have my last three-word special. Even if I never use it, it won't have been wasted. I'll have been thrilled at the possibility on occasions like that. I'm still mad about maple donuts, bowled over by the chalk cliffs, newborn babies and listening to Vivaldi, and was devoted to faithful Rover and dear old Bruno. A situation could still arise when I'll pull out my last chance but whoever the recipient is; new person, old friend or my husband back from his travels, the hearer will know he's hit the jackpot!

Susan Siddeley writes poetry and short stories. Hailing from Yorkshire, England, she strives to see the lighter side of everyday situations, especially where words and love are entwined.
Her memoir *Home First* was launched in October 2011

# Transcendence

In the summer of 2009, I was diagnosed with breast cancer. The initial diagnosis is the most difficult. There is shock. There is sadness. There is self-doubt. There is even some guilt and self-blame. My first instinct was to ask myself what I had done differently from other women who didn't have cancer. How could I have made this or let this happen? Given the circumstances, it is an irrational but "normal" question.

Our first instinct is to ask "Why?" This question would follow me for the duration of my treatment. I came to deep levels of understanding. Shit happens. We find a way around it. I've never believed that God gives you more than you can handle. At times I think that life is overwhelming. With cancer, the mind cannot even process the information for several weeks. The first one hundred days, they say, are the worst. There is no "why." That's the first thing I learned.

I decided I would find pockets of joy and moments of grace. Well I didn't really decide so much as plod along. I knew that if I just kept taking action, kept moving, stopping to cry as needed, I'd be okay. And I was. I treated myself kindly. I let myself be wherever this experience took me. I smashed some plates. I screamed. I think it saved my life. And my sanity.

Once I accepted that traditional treatment was the right choice for me, a middle-aged woman, it was time to take action. With two surgeries, chemotherapy and radiation it's quite the process. It's a physical rollercoaster, an emotional haunted house.

Difficult doesn't describe the journey. It's so hard, so profoundly frightening, that the darkness actually yields a very peaceful surrender. Just as the body goes into shock in a trauma, so does the soul. I gave in to the idea of dying, to live fully. I accepted the possibility of death and I chose to live life for however long that would be. Living fully would be my new project.

I learned so much. I learned how great the medical system is in Canada. I had the most wonderful, caring doctors and nurses. I experienced a tsunami of love from friends and family. They threw a fundraiser for me with a band. They called it the *Breast Party Ever!*

I had some difficult times, of course. Some friends became afraid and left. They said they were "here for you, anytime," then didn't return my calls. They squirmed when we met. The person I was dating left at this time. Fear does strange things. I lost a lot. I let go of a lot. It made room for so much more in my life. I let go of the woman I had been. I welcomed the woman I would become. I had a new and deep compassion. I developed the courage and grace that the journey back to health requires.

I spent a lot of time thinking about my life, where I wanted to go, where I had been. Had I any regrets? I spoke to many women who had felt the same way, thought the same thoughts. That's the thing about experience–there is this unspoken language. Yeah, I get it, the silence says. The specific words women used to support me didn't matter. They too knew that you can never go back to who you were. That "you" no longer exists. There is mourning. Then there is a morning. There is a letting go, the darkness, a newness, and the dawn of hope. As I lost my hair, I shed so much more of my old self. I came to a new understanding.

I no longer believe that my spirituality, my goodness, has a protective effect, that nothing bad will happen because I'm a deeply spiritual, kind, enlightened person. I now know that something terrible can happen, even to a great person. I also know I can survive it, and come out stronger on the other side.

This was the most profound learning: that bad stuff happens to really good people. More importantly, I now knew how to go through bad stuff in a more peaceful, accepting manner. I found a way to experience cancer for what it was, instead of projecting into a fearful future, or regretting some past. I stayed in the here and now, and dealt with only this moment.

For support, I called in the troops. I recruited all friends and family to support me. Some knew exactly what to do. I had to educate most people about what I needed. I first asked myself what I needed; Listening, A safe place to cry, Orange Tic Tacs, Acceptance. There's no doing it wrong with cancer. If I could share one thing, that would be it.

One day, I sat in a cafe with Deya, a relatively new friend. We talked about how difficult this experience might be as I prepared to go for chemo. I knew I would lose my hair. For a woman that is very difficult. Our hair is so much a part of our identity. I knew I would need a wig very soon.

She then did the most loving, unselfish thing. She offered to cut off her beautiful long dark hair so I could have my very own custom-made wig. But that wasn't all! Because her husband, Ulises, also had long dark hair; he offered his hair too! Their gesture was a testament to their unselfish love for each other and for me. I learned they had been growing their hair for this specific purpose and that they felt honored to offer it to someone they knew. In the end, I didn't go with a natural hair wig. It would have taken months to make one. That offer, however, and the love it represented helped get me through the next few difficult months of treatment. I kept asking myself, *Who gets an offer like that? Me! I'm so lucky!* Then I received another surprise; my friend Joyce, who owns a wig shop, gave me a private, discrete wig-fitting in her shop. With her loving expertise, she fitted me with two glamorous wigs.

The one thing I learned most about myself was my capacity for receiving love. I didn't know I would be able to be so vulnerable. I learned to receive love, a priceless gift. Where I felt broken, I allowed others to glue the pieces of my soul back together with their love. After treatment, I came together like a mosaic, different than my original form, yet even more beautiful when I took a step back and looked at the big picture. I feel deeply blessed by this experience.

# War and Love

My mother and father were Presbyterian missionaries in Puebla, Mexico where I was born in 1925. I always felt as if I wanted to get out and play with the other boys, but I found it impossible because they played much rougher than I was used to. From my parents I learned English and acquired much of my attitude. One of the biblical commandments that I remember is *Thou shalt love thy neighbour as thyself.* I wondered if that included Mexicans. Did my parents love them? Now, I believe that they did. They wanted to bring them into the twentieth century by teaching them that love and understanding would get them where they wanted to go. The hatred existing on both sides between Americans and Mexicans was fatal to any progress in life.

By the time I was sixteen and a student in Puebla, WWII had been ongoing for a few years and Uncle Sam was looking for lads from the United States to come and take part. Although I was too young and small for my age, I enlisted in spite of my parents' objections. I ran away from home and went up to Loreto, Texas to join the Marine Corps. When I arrived, the recruiting sergeant glared down at me.

"Boy, what are you doing here?" he asked. "You better be back home drinking milk out of a bottle."

That angered me.

"I came here to join the Marines," I replied.

He laughed.

"If you don't take me in the Marines I'm going to go somewhere else and join the army, and that'll show you," I said.

"No, lad, come here. I'm going to sign you up," he said. "Are you eighteen?"

"I'm lying. But I'm eighteen."

"How old are you?'

"Sixteen."

"You said you were eighteen, but I'll sign you up. Do you want to stay here and be my assistant?"

"No, I want to fight."

"All right, stupid."

The Marines flew me to Camp Lejeune in North Carolina. After sixteen weeks of training they considered us ready to go to war. I was a private. They'd shown us at least eight ways of killing a person. I excelled at rifle shooting because I'd hunted rabbits as a little kid. I quickly learned to fire a machine gun. Because I was such a short and small guy the other marines teased me with comments such as, "What are you going to do? Step on their toes and then shoot them?" By that time I was supposed to hate somebody but I couldn't figure out whom. I didn't want to kill anybody I didn't hate.

Then the Marines transferred us to the war zone in the Far East, on the Pacific island of Kwajalein where we joined the Fourth Marine Division. We came in as replacements for several casualties. There was a charge and every shot I fired clipped an enemy soldier. Another three weeks passed before we saw any more action. Then we became involved in a fire fight where the enemy ran away; we assumed it was a victory. I made the rank of sergeant. Risking my life for my country seemed the right thing to do. Now in my eighties, when I look back on it I think *Foster, you were stupid.* I fought in that war for two and a half years.

After the war, the Marines sent me to Yale University. I was the shortest man in my class. They wanted me to obtain a full education in International Relations so that I could become an officer. I went into the reserves and in 1950 I was called up for the

Korean War as a Platoon Commander. Too many of the captains had been killed, so I received a little training over a couple of weekends resulting in promotion as a captain. I decided that I would be the best possible officer that I could.

Now that I had charge of all those lives, I suddenly realized that I hadn't been a responsible person in the past. If my troops got hurt I had thought, *Well, tough.* If they got killed I had felt very, very sorry but figured they must have made a mistake. The responsibility for the lives of my men changed my attitude and I realized that, on the other side, the enemy must have the same kinds of feelings. *Am I supposed to shoot them or am I not supposed to shoot them?*

I considered the commandment *Thou shalt not kill.* I felt guilty in pressuring other people to kill quickly. I had been killing young men my age. I wondered how many would have made good teachers or become successful in whatever career they chose if I had just not bothered to go to war. I saw a counsellor who counselled many Marines. I stopped blabbing about being an ex-Marine.

I had slowly changed my thinking about killing. By the time I returned home, I had decided that I wanted to do the opposite, to enhance life in people. Religion was the answer as it had been for my parents. I was ordained a Presbyterian Reverend. I liked the work. Most of all I enjoyed visiting people if they had troubles, were sick or in jail. I listened to them and tried not to tell them what to do.

After I married, my wife and I lived in Mexico City for five years. During that time, we read in the newspapers about the CIA forming the Contras in Nicaragua. I traveled down to Nicaragua to volunteer as a translator in brokering mini accords between the Contras and the Sandinistas. I went from a man who fought in wars to one involved finding peace through mediation.

In my early fifties, I joined the Veterans for Peace. The organization burgeoned because many other veterans thought that war is evil and that it is wrong to kill people no matter who they are. Each year, on Veterans Day, I proudly don my medals and join them. My heart still remains with the Marines. I feel sorry for them. I feel connected to them. If it weren't for my age, my duty would be to go and teach them what not to do.

The best way to teach love is to show love. Rather than moving apart in fear and hatred, it is better to move together in love and reconciliation. I've had a change of heart.

www.ingramcontent.com/pod-product-compliance
Lightning Source LLC
Chambersburg PA
CBHW070015100426
42740CB00013B/2509